# PRAISE FOR
## The Back in Time Ta

Janet Boyer's groundbreaking system provides a
and using the Tarot. *Back in Time Tarot* is a signifi
for novice students and seasoned professionals alik

—Phyllis Vega, author of *Pow.. .... .. Romancing the Tarot*

Janet Boyer's BIT Method is a refreshing approach to Tarot. Her innovative
technique is user-friendly and yields amazing results. . . . I don't think I will ever
look at tarot cards the same!

—Lisa Hunt, author of *Animals Divine Tarot* and artist for *Fantastical Creatures Tarot*

What a great idea! The best way to learn Tarot is to live it. *Back in Time Tarot*
helps you do exactly that. Janet's BIT Method is a fun, unique approach to
relating the Tarot to our modern lives. Everyone should try it!

—Teresa Michelsen, author of *The Complete Tarot Reader* and
*Designing Your Own Tarot Spreads*

Janet's BIT Method is a superb experiential technique for both beginners and
seasoned professionals alike. Fun yet deeply thought provoking, *Back in Time
Tarot* really hits the spot!

—Josephine Ellershaw, author of *Easy Tarot*

Janet Boyer's *Back in Time Tarot* is wonderful.

—Wilma Carroll, author of *The 2-Hour Tarot Tutor*

Janet's BIT Method is a wonderful guide in introducing the reader to a
fantastic Tarot adventure.

—Nina Lee Braden, author of *Tarot for Self Discovery*

I find *Back in Time Tarot* a truly valuable addition to Tarot literature and yet
another proof of the Tarot's ability to constantly generate new ideas and perspectives.

—Philip Carr-Gomm, author of *The Druid Craft, The Druid Plant Oracle,
The Druid Animal Oracle,* and *Sacred Spaces*

It is truly original.

—Chris Butler, illustrator of five Tarot decks, including the highly
anticipated *Quantum Tarot* by Kunati

This fresh, original approach to experiencing the cards is as fun as it is
informative. Tarot enthusiasts of all levels will find the BIT Method a valuable
technique to add to their Tarot education and practice.

—Ruth Ann and Wald Amberstone, directors of the Tarot School and
authors of *Tarot Tips* and *The Secret Language of Tarot*

Packed full of a fascinating range of contributions from a virtual "who's who" of the Tarot world, this is a must read for those wanting to make their Tarot experience both more personal and more profound.

—Karen Mahony, Tarot author and creator of *The Victorian Romantic Tarot, The Baroque Bohemian Cats' Tarot, The Bohemian Gothic Tarot,* and many other decks

The Back in Time (BIT) Method . . . is a wonderfully refreshing approach to Tarot that any reader or Tarot enthusiast will just be itching to try themselves!

—Emily Carding, creator and artist of *The Transparent Tutor*

Reading Janet Boyer's *Back in Time Tarot* is like talking tarot with a good friend. . . . I found Janet's book fascinating and refreshing, and I can't wait to apply the BIT Method to my readings.

—Kay Stopforth, creator of *Quantum Tarot* and author of its companion book

Both newcomers and masters can benefit from this method, and it even works for those that don't believe!

—Monicka Clio Sakki, creator and artist of *The Sakki-Sakki Tarot*

Whatever your level of Tarot expertise, after reading this book, you'll gain valuable new perspectives on the cards.

—James Ricklef, award-winning author of *Tarot Tells the Tale* and *Tarot: Get the Whole Story,* as well as the creator of the deck, *Tarot of the Masters*

Janet Boyer's *Back in Time Tarot* Book is a groundbreaking new way to use Tarot to add meaning and make sense of our lives.

—Kat Black, creator of the popular and critically acclaimed *Golden Tarot* and the forthcoming *Touchstone Tarot*

Janet Boyer's BIT Method uses the power of choice to help you explore the cards and your life in new ways. It hass become a welcome addition to my Tarot toolkit.

—Joan Bunning, author of *Learning the Tarot, Learning Tarot Reversals,* and *Learning Tarot Spreads*

I can think of no better way to make the essence of Tarot archetypes instantly relevant to the world around us than the exercises found in Janet Boyer's marvelous book.

—Lon Milo DuQuette, author of *Understanding Aleister Crowley's Thoth Tarot*

Janet Boyer's *Back in Time Tarot* not only opens a new way of understanding Tarot but of storytelling itself.

—Elizabeth Cunningham, author of *Wild Mercy: Tarot Inspired Musings,* The Maeve Chronicles, and counselor in private practice

# The Back in Time Tarot Book

## Tarot Book

Picture the Past, Experience the Cards, Understand the Present

JANET BOYER

for the evolving human spirit

## HAMPTON ROADS
PUBLISHING COMPANY, INC.

Cover design by Steve Amarillo
Cover art © Nova Development Corporation

Card images from the Universal Waite Tarot deck © U.S. Games Systems, Inc.
Used with permission.

Hampton Roads Publishing Company, Inc.
1125 Stoney Ridge Road
Charlottesville, VA 22902

434-296-2772
fax: 434-296-5096
e-mail: hrpc@hrpub.com
www.hrpub.com

If you are unable to order this book from your local bookseller, you may order directly
from the publisher.
Call 1-800-766-8009, toll-free.

Library of Congress Cataloging-in-Publication Data

Boyer, Janet.
  The back in time tarot book : picture the past, experience the cards,
understand the present / Janet Boyer.
      p. cm.
  Includes bibliographical references and index.
  Summary: "A new method for reading the tarot. Using almost any tarot deck and a
memory from their past, readers can gain understanding of their present and insight
into their future"--Provided by publisher.
  ISBN 978-1-57174-587-3 (7 x 9 tp : alk. paper)
1. Tarot. I. Title.

  BF1879.T2B69 2008
  133.3'2424--dc22

                              2008030555

ISBN 978-1-57174-587-3
10 9 8 7 6 5 4 3 2 1
Printed on acid-free paper in Canada

*For my two guys, Ron and Noah,*
*two-thirds of the Three Musketeers and*
*the Huna Chukas*

# Contents

*continued*

# Foreword

Janet Boyer has read more Tarot books and seen more Tarot decks than anyone I know, so when she told me that she was writing a book of her own, I knew it was going to be something special. Her Back in Time (BIT) Method was even more amazing than I thought it would be—so amazing, in fact, that at first I didn't get it, just like the first time I tried to play the guitar or, for that matter, the first time I tried to learn to read Tarot cards.

Making music and learning to read Tarot cards have changed my life in wondrous ways—made my life what it is, actually—so I'm not one to let a little thing like not "getting" something stop me in my quest and, after reading through the book, I've got it and I love it!

Janet's inventive method benefits both novice and experienced Tarot readers. I actually consider myself both a novice (compared to where I will be in the future) and an expert—you've heard the expression "Zen mind, beginners mind!" There's nothing better to shake an expert in any subject out of their complacency and comfort level than a completely new way of looking at their area of expertise, and that is what Janet's Back in Time Method has done for me. The list of Tarot authors and artists in this book who've contributed their own experiences with Janet's BIT Method reads like a veritable Who's Who of today's exciting Tarot world, and I'm sure they'd agree with me that giving her BIT Method a whirl produced some unexpected insights and deep learning—and fun!

It's the greatest time in the history of Tarot to be a reader. I really think that in our lifetime we're going to see the disappearance of the ages-old negative associations of Tarot as occult and problematic to religious people. The computer age has so many benefits, and one that I've been availing myself of lately is explaining my attitude regarding reading Tarot cards as a variation on using a search engine like Google: you want to know something so you ask your question with the intention to receive the information you're looking for, all the while knowing that you're going to have to figure out which of the many answers you're going to receive is the right one. People seem to finally "get it" when I put it that way.

Janet Boyer's Back in Time Method allows everyone desirous of sharpening their intuitive inner "search engine" to give real meaning to the cards of whichever Tarot deck they choose to work with. It's also one of the best methods I can imagine to help a newcomer to our ancient art decide on which deck to use—not surprising coming from the Queen of Tarot's encyclopedic understanding of the hundreds of Tarot decks available!

For newcomer and expert alike, working backward from an event we think we know can help give new meanings to our Tarot deck, while at the same time offering valuable glimpses into our subconscious assumptions, unexamined beliefs, and suppressed issues.

Quantum physics postulates that there is no reason why time can't flow backward, so that makes Janet's Back in Time Tarot Method not only thoroughly enjoyable and illuminating, but scientifically based, too! If

you're like me, I'm sure you're going to spend many hours working with the BIT Method. Like the Tarot itself, using it on a regular basis will answer your every question, increase in your intuitive abilities, and produce extraordinary life experiences.

*—Monte Farber,*

author of *The Enchanted Tarot, The Zerner/Farber Deck,*

*The Instant Tarot Reader, True Love Tarot,* and

*The Tarot Discovery Kit*

(www.TheEnchantedWorld.com)

# *Preface*

Hello, and welcome to a grand adventure starring you and a deck of cards called the Tarot!

Perhaps you're reading this preface in a bookstore, trying to decide if this book is for you, or maybe reading a sample chapter of the book online. You may be intrigued by the Tarot but at the same time apprehensive because of the spooky—and sometimes outlandish—film portrayals of both the cards and those who use them. If so, I understand completely.

Not only was I raised in a fundamentalist religious tradition, but I was also a practicing ordained minister. At one time, I was simultaneously fascinated and repelled by divination tools like Tarot. By divination, I mean methods for accessing information and insight through physical means, such as palm reading, runes, dreams, and so on. I was repelled because, although the religious denomination I was involved with taught and practiced forms of divination such as prophecy and bibliomancy (obtaining spiritual insight and guidance by randomly selecting portions of the Bible), other tools like Tarot were deemed evil. Eventually, I came to the realization that a Tarot deck is, essentially, a stack of paper. There's nothing threatening about a stack of paper. Ultimately, I was the one who imbued these cards with meaning and purpose. And for me, this purpose included the desire to use the Tarot to connect with

God, nourish my spirit, gain insight into life lessons, illuminate options, and deliver messages of hope to humanity. After all, the Tarot does not exist in a vacuum, and its application is something that I could determine for myself.

So how did I end up going from being a Christian minister to a Tarot reader, expert, and author? Ever since I was a young girl, I inexplicably knew things about people and situations—what some would call psychic. In Pentecostal circles, however, the term used was "prophet," a word that comes from the Hebrew *nabi*, which translates as "mouthpiece." The messages delivered to individuals or groups were considered prophecies, a practice taught in the Bible and considered acceptable—even desirable—in the Pentecostal and Charismatic religious traditions within which I taught and ministered.

One day, through a sermon delivered by a traveling minister called an evangelist, I had an epiphany that there was no literal hell. Period. Being an independent scholar, I had to verify my spiritual revelation with Biblical tradition, hermeneutics, and the original languages of the Bible. I soon discovered there was, indeed, evidence that no literal hell existed and that hell was merely a symbolic reference to experiencing separation from God.

My new way of thinking caused my church friends and ministerial colleagues to break all ties with me, effectively excommunicating me from both spiritual service and their homes. (You'll learn more about my experience in my BIT snapshot titled "No Hell.") Although I found myself on the outside of my familiar religious path, the knack for receiving and decoding information beyond the five senses never left me. How was I to continue using this gift outside of the church? Eventually, I felt moved to buy a computer, create a Web site, post articles online, and reach out to humanity. Through my labor of love, I eventually became the New Age editor at the second largest women's site on the Web. It was during these years that Tarot came across my path, and I decided to begin to explore this tool for its psychological, self-help, and spiritual merits, especially in terms of helping others. Over time, I became a Tarot deck and book reviewer, even rising to the level of an Amazon.com Top 100 Reviewer. In addition, I'm also a Tarot columnist for *Tarot World Magazine* and a Tarot editor for several publications.

Ideas for my articles and writings often come during unexpected moments, most often during times of relaxation. In the spring of 2007, I spontaneously took a bubble bath in the middle of the day. While bright sunlight filtered through the bathroom window, I "zoned out," enjoying the warm water and my view of the budding branches that swayed in the breeze. Out of the blue, I "heard" the phrase "back in time" in my head. Then, in what I can only describe as a cosmic download from the Universe, I received a flood of information on how to create a method for experiencing the Tarot "backward."

Now, before this surreal "aha" moment, I had paired people, memories, stories, and events with Tarot cards, but only in my head. I hadn't shared my process with anyone, let alone written about it. But this bathtub revelation actually organized the process into a specific method that begins with you, the individual, and then flows outward to the cards, rather than beginning with a list of card meanings that you must memorize first in order to work with a Tarot deck (a premise of many Tarot books). I realized that our memories and immediate experiences are laden with emotional content and sensory data. Deconstructing memories and then consciously choosing Tarot cards to represent their components can forge a deeply personal link between a person and individual cards.

Through my writing and reviewing, I knew many Tarot authors and deck artists. Shortly after the revelation in the bathtub, it seemed natural to call upon my friends and colleagues to collaborate on this new baby that wanted to be birthed. While I was excited to begin creating Back in Time (BIT) Snapshots for this book, it occurred to me that having multiple writers offer their unique takes on a single method (something that has never been done before) would not only make for an interesting book, but also show readers how easy, fun, and illuminating the Tarot can be with the BIT Method. Intrigued and inspired, these renowned Tarot authors and artists tapped into their memories to formulate heartfelt BIT Snapshots that range from poignant to comical, frustrating to magical. What surprised me in their feedback were their remarks about how innovative and perspective-altering the BIT Method was for them as they went through the process. I was surprised because these respected authors and deck creators have seen countless Tarot methods, books, and decks over the years.

For example, artist Ann Cass used her own *WorldTree Tarot* deck for her BIT Snapshot "You Can Catch a Robin If You Put Salt on Its Tail." She told me that she would never have considered pairing a card with something as innocuous as a saltshaker if it weren't for the BIT Method. By pondering a childhood memory, however, breaking it down into its components, and then consciously pairing them with Tarot cards, she uncovered new insights into that memory, as well as insights on the King of Wands from her own deck (the card she paired with the saltshaker).

After working on her BIT Snapshots—one about emerging a stronger, more confident woman after the pain of divorce and the other about overcoming creator's block—award-winning artist and author Lisa Hunt shared how valuable and cathartic the BIT Method was for her. She told me that she would never look at Tarot cards the same way again (and she is an artist who has painted five entire Tarot decks!).

So whether you're entirely new to Tarot or a veteran of the cards, my BIT Method offers you thrilling discoveries as you rummage through your memory banks, sift through historical events, overhear conversations, ponder great stories, and watch the news, and then pair these scenarios with the Tarot cards of your choice.

# Acknowledgments

Thanks first and foremost to the Unseen Helpers—those glorious agents of the Divine—who inspire, encourage, strengthen, and provide in myriad unexpected ways. A complicated secret handshake to Jesus, who has never left me nor refused to speak with me. If only some people knew how much you ROCK!

Much appreciation goes to Mark McElroy, who sent off his Back in Time (BIT) Snapshot within one hour of my request and provided great feedback with his practiced eye.

Heartfelt thanks to Judika Illes, who saw something special in the few files I sent to her and offered to show them to Greg Brandenburgh at Hampton Roads. Speaking of Greg: Thanks for setting off peals of laughter with your snarky wit, as well as for your marketing acumen. "Let go . . . and let Greg." Water signs rule!

Special thanks to my friends and colleagues who so generously shared their time, enthusiasm, and BIT Snapshots: Teresa Michelsen, Wilma Carroll, Phyllis Vega, Josephine Ellershaw, Joan Bunning, Lisa Hunt, Nina Lee Braden, Mary K. Greer, Ann Cass, Riccardo Minetti, Zach Wong, Elizabeth Cunningham, and Lon Milo DuQuette. Their unique takes on my BIT Method help bring it to life!

Hugs and a standing ovation to Monte Farber, a highly perceptive psychic and talented wordsmith, who makes up one half of the enchanted couple (the other half being the lovely award-winning artist, Amy Zerner). Through their Enchanted World, Monte and Amy have gifted humanity with colorful, vibrant, and accessible "spiritual power tools"—enriching my life and many others with their unique brand of compassionate, incisive wisdom. Thank you, Monte, for your sincere and enthusiastic foreword to this book. I so much appreciate your time and thoughtfulness.

Rousing applause for my warm, astute, intuitive, and exacting Capricorn editor, Amy Rost. I've always wondered why authors thanked their editors so heartily. Now I know! You are a shining jewel of a person, and I appreciate your cheerleading, patience, and tact during the editing process. In addition to your outstanding suggestions and insights, you took on the role of "the reader," making sure I filled in the gaps and stayed faithful to my original intention for this book.

Sincerest thanks to U.S. Games founder/publisher Stuart Kaplan for his kind permission to use the Universal Waite images for *The Back in Time Tarot Book*.

Thanks to Tania Seymour, production editor at Hampton Roads Publishing, for ably shepherding my book through the copy-editing, typesetting, and proofing processes. You're a pleasure to chat with! Also, many thanks to all the talented people at Hampton Roads Publishing who work behind the scenes to make *Back in Time Tarot* a success.

A big shout out to two majorly talented designers: Steve Amarillo, who designed the lovely (and oh-so-fitting) cover for my book; and Rick Bickhart, whose graceful attention to detail forms the elegant interior layout and illustrations for *Back in Time Tarot*. You two have surpassed my grandest imaginings of what a beautiful book should look like!

Gratitude to three outstanding English teachers: Nancy Masuga, my tenth grade English teacher; Rose Gabeletto, my eleventh grade English teacher; and Laura Brookins, my college English professor. Mrs. Masuga introduced me to the dazzling realm of symbol and metaphor, a world I never quite left. Mrs. Gabeletto and Professor Brookins taught me how to "slash and burn" my rambling prose, which stung at the time but (eventually) helped me become a tighter writer. Thank you, all.

Thanks to Lisa Shea, founder, Webmaster, and senior editor of BellaOnline.com, for giving me the opportunity to serve as the New Age editor for two years. It was her suggestion to write reviews that likely veered me to the fulfilling writing path I now tread.

Appreciation to Heidi Snelgrove, founder of TWM Publishing, for giving me a regular BIT Snapshot column in *Tarot World Magazine*. She has gone from employer to friend in a very short time span.

To my fans, Internet friends, and faithful readers: Thank you for all the kind e-mails, supportive posts, and silent prayers that you've sent my way over the years. Many blessings to you!

Lastly, deep gratitude and hugs to my wonderful husband, Ron, for his unfailing support and encouragement of this book (as with all my wild ideas and projects). My soul mate and best friend stands ready after a hard day's work to help me when I need it, and I can't tell you how much that means to me. Always ready with a kind word, shoulder rub, or cup of coffee, he's proof positive that it's actually an *angel* that's in the details! And to my precious Zhoomie—my son, Noah. Sweetheart, your cootie catcher was *right!* This book *did* get published! Thank you for all your hugs, kisses, and exclamations of "Love ya, Mom!" while I worked.

Oh, and I can't forget the snuggle buddies, our cats Neo and Stewart (a.k.a. Tom and Yam). Thanks for the cuddles and warmth, sleepy kitties. You'll get more lap time now that Mama is done with this book!

# Introduction

No matter who we are or where we live, we all have one thing in common: a past.

You know that last sentence you just read, the one about the universal thing we all have in common? It's already in the past!

It just so happens that the past—whether one second or hundreds of years ago—serves as the basis for an innovative, easy-to-use technique for experiencing the Tarot: my Back in Time (BIT) Method. The BIT Method relies on two elements: a deck of cards and a snapshot, which can be a memory of any past event but can also include stories from movies, literature, and television shows; historical events; biographical details; or pop-culture and news reports scrolling at the bottom of the TV screen. The BIT Method is the process of recalling your snapshot and consciously pairing the components with Tarot cards. The result of this engaging process—the full picture, if you will—is what I term a **BIT Snapshot**, a completed picture of the pairing of Tarot cards with your snapshot.

For example, in this book, I apply the BIT Method to a snapshot of the familiar classic German folktale "Cinderella." I break this beloved story down into components—such as Cinderella's father, the magical white bird, and the festival where she meets the prince—and then select cards that I feel best represent each of those elements from my perspective.

Notice that I said the BIT Method is a technique for *experiencing* the Tarot, not learning it. I make this distinction because, unlike some Tarot books, this one doesn't require you to memorize hundreds of complicated, esoteric card meanings. Instead, it shows you how to connect to the cards on your own terms, in a way that makes your favorite Tarot deck (or decks) truly your own. By pairing your memories—the past—with Tarot cards via the BIT Method, you begin to make practical, helpful associations with the characters and symbols depicted in card imagery. Memories, world events, and stirring stories are anchored into your consciousness through emotion and sensory impressions. By connecting various components of the past with particular cards, you will eventually create a powerful, personal set of card associations that will stick with you over time. In the future, should you then select or encounter a Tarot card you've bonded with via the BIT Method, your subjective associations will come to mind. The more associations you make by using the "Your Turn" exercises at the end of the BIT Snapshots in this book and by formulating your own BIT Snapshots, the greater the breadth and depth of your individualized card meanings. Like the Fool portrayed in most Tarot decks, you'll be carrying a metaphorical pouch over your shoulder as you practice the BIT Method, collecting various associations to access for future Tarot readings, personal contemplation, spiritual guidance, journaling, or even creative writing.

Whether you are completely new to Tarot or are an experienced Tarotist, the BIT Method will forever change the way you look at Tarot cards. By inviting you to experiment and play with your memories of past events, as well as scenes from history, the news, pop culture, and other sources, the BIT Method offers you new ways of looking at both life and the Tarot.

If you are a new student of the Tarot, the BIT Method allows you to begin with a blank slate and affords you the opportunity to get to know a particular deck intimately. Many Tarot beginners are overwhelmed at the prospect of learning at least seventy-eight card meanings in order to feel comfortable with a deck. By approaching Tarot with a sense of play and curiosity, however, as the BIT Method does, you can make friends with the cards in a relaxed and entertaining manner. If you're an intermediate to advanced student of the Tarot, the BIT Method will refine the meanings you've currently assigned to each card as well as increase your cache of associations.

No matter what your level of experience, the BIT Method will broaden and deepen your understanding of both Tarot and life itself. In fact, the card associations you make using this technique will not only help you achieve additional insights, but also inform your present and your future. For example, you may use the BIT Method to understand a troubling or perplexing situation that has occurred. By examining this situation through the lens of Tarot, you will be able to zoom out for a big picture view of the people, conversations, and thoughts involved. This new way of seeing provides some objectivity to a personal experience, which can then provide much-needed answers for you in the present. And, should you gain wisdom, insight, and compassion from the process, you may very well carry this knowledge into your future choices, attitudes, and expectations.

In addition to these benefits, utilizing the BIT Method will increase and sharpen your innate intuitive abilities. The Tarot contains a rich system of symbols and archetypes, and by connecting your personal stories to the cards, you'll be tapping into universal knowledge. As author Shakti Gawain notes, "The intuitive mind draws on the information gathered through personal experience and also on the deep, infinite storehouse of knowledge and wisdom known as the universal mind." The more you employ the BIT Method, the greater your capacity to access that universal mind which includes the world of myth and collective archetypes. When you come across similar situations or portrayals of certain motifs often found in fairy tales and movies, you'll make connections that will likely stay with you throughout your life, especially if you take time to record them in a journal.

Part 1 of this book gives you all the information you need to get started using the BIT Method. Chapter 1 offers some basic background on the Tarot. In chapter 2, I go through the BIT Method in detail and give you a sample BIT Snapshot that illustrates the steps of creating one.

For part 2, my colleagues and I have created dozens of BIT Snapshots for you to enjoy. Chapter 3, "Personal Experiences," contains compelling BIT Snapshots based on personal milestones, challenging situations, and everyday occurrences. Dealing with the boss from hell, a child flying the coop, chronic migraines, and the aftermath of 9/11 are all here, as are scenarios involving an unexpected Christmas gift, a Tarot reading in Italy, and a strange incident at a park. Chapter 4, "Literature, TV, and Movies," provides snapshots of stories such as "Cinderella," *Of Mice and Men, The Wizard of Oz,* and *The Grinch Who Stole Christmas,* while chapter five, "Headlines and History," offers BIT Snapshots based on the world scene. In this chapter, you'll find

BIT Snapshots on Paris Hilton, the BTK serial killer, inventor Alexander Graham Bell, and the Crocodile Hunter, Steve Irwin. Chapter 6, "Odds and Ends," offers an eclectic mix of BIT Snapshots based on pop songs from the 1980s, holidays, and U.S. states.

By reading our BIT Snapshots, you'll get a feel for the various approaches to the BIT Method and the reasoning behind our choices for the Tarot cards we picked to match our memories, stories, and historical events. You'll get to see how each of us stretched our imaginations and intuition to choose the story components we did, the card choices we made, and, most important, why we chose particular cards to match the components.

To see the wide range of personal associations given to the same cards is utterly fascinating. For example, in Phyllis Vega's BIT Snapshot "Selling House," she associates the Ten of Pentacles with the "ultimate in financial security and firm foundations for a contented family life." Mary K. Greer, in her BIT Snapshot "Discovering the Tarot," chose the same card to represent "the sense of a family home at Christmas" and an "intriguing gift from a near stranger." But in my BIT Snapshot "Songs from the 1980s," I correlate the song "Our House" by Madness with the Ten of Pentacles, too, but my take on this card is more sinister. Sometimes it's clear to see why a person chose the particular card they did; other times, a person's card pairings within the BIT Snapshots seem to be an enigma—utterly personal and not based on card imagery alone.

After each BIT Snapshot, I provide a commentary that expands on the author's card choices. This segment supplies background information on certain cards and decks, as well as common Tarot practices and alternative perspectives. So, although the main focus of this book isn't Tarot history and tradition, you will still acquire informative tidbits to expand your knowledge. Because I'm a teacher at heart (and a trivia lover), I've also included some little-known facts in both my BIT Snapshots and the commentary sections.

The BIT Snapshots and the commentary are not telling you, "This is the way you *must* see these Tarot cards both now and in the future." (Many Tarot books that offer traditional card meanings, backed by Tarot "experts," do seem to say that, and thus they can keep you from creating your own card associations.) Instead, seeing the various ways others use the BIT Method and view the cards will inspire confidence in your own ability to recognize what is important to *you* in the cards.

The "Your Turn" exercises after each BIT Snapshot invite you to practice the BIT Method immediately by recalling your own stories and making your own associations. The exercises consist of three questions that encourage you to recall a similar event, story, or person and to select cards to correspond to the components. The first question asks you to create a BIT Snapshot from something that you've experienced firsthand. The second question invites you to recall something that you've witnessed as a third party, and the last one prods you to recall events from history, the news, and pop culture.

Although the Tarot is a visual medium, I've decided not to show every card from every deck mentioned in the BIT Snapshots for practical reasons. (Can you image how big this book would be with hundreds of cards from more than forty Tarot decks referenced?) If you would enjoy seeing the exact cards and decks described in each BIT Snapshot, however, you can visit my Web site, www.JanetBoyer.com, and click on the "BIT Book" tab on the navigation

no longer available 2/2024.

menu to the left or, alternatively, on the *Back in Time Tarot* book-cover icon. Also, all seventy-eight cards from the entire *Universal Waite Tarot* are pictured at the back of this book, which will give you a feel for the cards chosen by each contributor. Since many decks referenced in this book are Rider-Waite inspired, you'll get a good feel for the impressions evoked by the cards.

Personally, I never tire of creating BIT Snapshots. Every time I use the BIT Method, I employ my intuitive abilities, cultivate my observational skills, broaden my cache of card associations, and deepen my love for Tarot. I believe the BIT Method not only makes me a better Tarot reader, but also aids me in becoming a more self-aware and compassionate person. It is my hope that after reading *Back in Time Tarot*, you'll find the same to be true for you.

Are you up for a stimulating journey using the Tarot and the BIT Method? If so, then have a seat, begin to read, and let's start our voyage together!

# GETTING
# STARTED

THE MAGICIAN.

IX

THE HERMIT.

# Getting to Know the Tarot

## AN OVERVIEW OF TAROT STRUCTURE

For those of you completely new to Tarot, let me briefly explain Tarot structure. A typical Tarot deck contains seventy-eight cards. The **Major Arcana** (also known as Trumps) are twenty-two cards typically numbered from 0 to 21 and named to match the imagery they depict. Cards from the Majors include the Fool, the Magician, the Lovers, the Hermit, the Wheel of Fortune, the Moon, the Sun, and the World. Some deck creators rename the Trumps; for example, the *Oracle Tarot* substitutes a card called Tradition for the Hierophant and one called Bondage for the Devil.

The **Minor Arcana** consist of forty cards that are much like a deck of playing cards because they're organized in four suits numbered from ace to ten.

**Wands,** the suit usually associated with the element fire, may also be called staves, rods, batons, or clubs.

**Cups,** usually associated with the element water, may also be called chalices, vessels, cauldrons, or hearts.

**Swords,** usually associated with the element air, may also be called blades or spades.

**Pentacles,** usually associated with the element earth, may also be called coins, stones, crystals, disks, or diamonds.

Some deck designers get quite creative in naming the suits, especially with theme decks. For example, the suits in the *Halloween Tarot* are imps (fire), bats (air), ghosts (water), and pumpkins (earth). Another example is the *Osho Zen Tarot*, which names the earth suit rainbows and the air suit clouds. In the *True Love Tarot* deck, the fire suit is roses, the water suit shells, the air suit wings, and the earth suit gems.

The sixteen **court cards** (four for each suit) are often called pages, knights, queens, and kings. Some decks, such as the *Quest Tarot*, use attributions such as sons, daughters, mothers, and fathers. The *World Spirit Tarot* labels them seers, seekers, sibyls, and sages. The *DruidCraft Tarot* and other decks have princesses, princes, queens, and kings. The *Oracle Tarot* forgoes court cards altogether.

## Choosing a Tarot Deck

These days, there are literally thousands of Tarot decks on the market. Some chain bookstores carry Tarot decks, as do independent metaphysical bookstores. Most decks stocked at brick-and-mortar bookstores are sealed, preventing you from seeing the actual cards before you buy them. In this case, or if you live in a rural area like mine with nary a New Age bookstore in sight, you may have to rely on the Internet for previewing cards and acquiring Tarot decks. Web sites that provide deck reviews accompanied by card images (such as my own Web site, www.JanetBoyer.com) can be especially valuable when you are searching for a Tarot deck. Amazon.com happens to be my favorite place on the Net to shop for both Tarot decks and books.

For the Back in Time (BIT) Method, you'll want to use a deck that has an illustrated Minor Arcana. This means that the numbered cards of each suit depict people and scenes rather than just suit symbols, such as actual cups or swords.

Artist Pamela Colman Smith, under the direction of Arthur E. Waite, had an uncanny knack for capturing ambiguous situations and emotion when drawing the images for the *Rider-Waite Tarot*. Rider and Sons was the company that originally published the deck in 1909, which is why the deck is referred to as the Rider-Waite. In homage to the previously oft-forgotten artist, many Tarotists now refer to the Rider-Waite deck as the Rider-Waite-Smith Tarot, or RWS for short. Because the Rider-Waite is one of the most influential deck designs in the world of Tarot, many artists and deck creators understandably use Rider-Waite imagery as a basis for their own designs. For example, just as the Rider-Waite shows the Magician standing before a table lined with symbols of the four elements, one arm raised with a finger pointing skyward and the other hand pointing downward, many deck artists portray similar imagery. Decks illustrated in the spirit of the Rider-Waite are often called Rider-Waite clones because of the card-for-card resemblance. Two fine Rider-Waite–inspired decks are the lively *Sharman-Caselli Tarot*, conceived by Juliet Sharman-Burke and illustrated by Giovanni Caselli, and the gorgeous, gilt-edged *Golden Tarot* by Kat Black.

Interestingly, there are also several versions of the Rider-Waite deck; the differences between them are mostly based on coloring. For example, Frankie Albano colored the *Albano-Waite Tarot*, while Mary Hanson-Roberts colored the *Universal Waite Tarot*. With its soft tones, the Universal Waite deck happens to be my personal favorite and the deck I used in most of my BIT Snapshots. Because of the ambiguity of the scenes and animated countenances of the figures, any version of the Rider-Waite deck that you're drawn to would be a good choice to use with the BIT Method, as would any of the Rider-Waite–inspired (or clone) decks.

Many other decks use images that bear little resemblance to Rider-Waite imagery, instead drawing inspiration from a wide variety of cultures, religious paths, esoteric traditions, mythology, pastimes, art movements, works of literature, and even movies, rock music, or comic books. As long as a deck speaks to you and depicts imagery that you can easily connect to memories and events, it would be a fine deck to use with the BIT Method.

In addition to the *Sharman-Caselli Tarot, Universal Waite Tarot,* and the *Golden Tarot,* a few of my favorite decks that work well with the BIT Method include the *Lisa Hunt Fairytale Tarot, Victorian Romantic Tarot,* and *Pictorial Key Tarot.*

For other good choices that have the added bonus of benign renderings of the Devil and Death cards, here are some other favorites (for more information, see "Tarot Decks Referenced in This Book" in the bibliography):

- *Baroque Bohemian Cats' Tarot*
- *Bright Idea Deck*
- *DruidCraft Tarot*
- *Gilded Tarot*
- *Halloween Tarot*
- *Housewives Tarot*
- *Hudes Tarot*
- *Mystic Faerie Tarot*
- *Oracle Tarot*
- *Vanessa Tarot*
- *Whimsical Tarot*
- *WorldTree Tarot*

The BIT Snapshots presented in *The Back in Time Tarot Book* use cards from more than forty decks. To see the actual cards used for each BIT Snapshot, please visit www.JanetBoyer.com and click on the "BIT Book" tab or the book's cover image.

# REVERSED AND COMBINED CARDS

In addition to deriving meaning from upright cards, some Tarot enthusiasts read reversed cards, often interpreting upside-down images as:

- Opposite of the upright meaning
- The upright meaning taken to an extreme
- An obstruction
- Negativity
- Waning influence
- In potential or about to come on the scene
- The same as the upright meaning but with less impact

I've chosen not to use reversals to create BIT Snapshots in this book as a matter of practicality and simplicity. Although addressing reversals in a comprehensive manner is beyond the scope of this book, I recommend *The Complete Book of Tarot Reversals*, by Mary K. Greer, or *Learning Tarot Reversals*, by Joan Bunning, if you'd like to explore the use of reversed cards.

Sometimes the nuance of a situation or person is better captured using two or more cards in concert. For example, although someone may choose the Lovers card alone to represent a marriage, I may choose, because of my personal associations, the Hierophant (a clergyman) plus the Two of Cups (romance) to represent a church ceremony, or the Two of Cups, Three of Cups (celebration), and Four of Wands (a pastoral scene) to represent an outdoor ceremony with lots of friends and family. For a marriage in front of a justice of the peace, I might choose the Two of Cups and Justice (often a card showing the "scales of justice," representing the legal system). The Two of Cups, the High Priestess, and the Four of Wands might reflect a pagan ceremony. The Knight of Cups (a proposal), the Eight of Wands (speed), and the Lovers (contracts or marriage) could depict an elopement. The keywords in parentheses in these examples are my own associations, and I include them to give you examples of how you can use card combinations to represent a component of the past if one card doesn't seem sufficient. A few of the BIT Snapshots use card combinations to represent one aspect of a memory or story, but the majority pair only one card per component.

## THE LIGHT/SHADOW CONTINUUM

In *Back in Time Tarot*, I've decided to approach the cards on a light/dark continuum. Seemingly positive cards can have a dark side, and seemingly difficult cards can have a bright side. For example, the Nine of Cups can indicate merriment or even wish fulfillment, but on the other end of the continuum, it can indicate drunkenness or gluttony.

Another example is the Three of Swords. Although this card often depicts a heart impaled by three blades, often seen as indicating heartache or failed romance, the image can also represent a much-needed release of pent-up emotions (including grief). The Rider-Waite image might even remind someone of the Three Musketeers, friends who stick together through both good times and extraordinary challenges. The BIT Method can help you realize where you see specific cards of your own preferred Tarot deck (or decks) falling on the light/shadow continuum.

# 2

# *How to Use the* BIT *Method*

## WHAT YOU'LL NEED

You need only two items to do the Back in Time (BIT) Method: the Tarot deck of your choice and a mental "snapshot," such as a memory or scenario from pop culture. If you grew up in the 1970s, as I did, you may remember those instant cameras that snapped a scene and spit out a picture that developed right before your eyes. Just as those cameras captured a moment in time, your mind can freeze any memory, movie, story, conversation, or historical event so you can re-create it using Tarot cards.

I recommend that you also pick up a notebook or journal to record your back-in-time scenario and the cards you choose to create your BIT Snapshot. By recording your correlations between past situations and Tarot cards, you will create a treasure trove that you can mine for future readings or simply use for expanding your self-awareness. The BIT Method is simple enough to perform in your head, but because you're unlikely to be able to recall all of the associations you make with the cards over time, I recommend recording scenarios and card associations in a BIT Method journal. (This journal could be an actual journal, a blank tablet, index cards, or loose-leaf pages placed in a folder or three-ring binder.) If you prefer journaling on a computer, you can record your BIT Snapshots by using a word-processing program or even in a personal online blog.

The original snapshot that you use can be an event from the distant past, if you'd like—such as the first Christmas you can remember—but you can also use a snapshot of something that happened to you five minutes ago. Events can range from momentous occasions, like graduating from high school, to more mundane situations, like taking your car to the mechanic for an inspection. Snapshots can also be situations that you've witnessed, such as an amusing exchange between a department-store clerk and a shopper or a current event that has just scrolled across the ticker on a twenty-four-hour news channel. You can use a historical event as a snapshot, or, if you're a fan of celebrity gossip, you could even use scenarios found in your favorite pop-culture magazine or tabloid. Your snapshot could even be a dream you had one night or a favorite movie, book, or song. The possibilities are only as limited as your imagination.

## WHAT TO DO

There are two basic ways you can approach creating a BIT Snapshot. In the first option, write down a list of the individual components of the snapshot. (Don't feel obligated to include every little detail as a component; the BIT Method is intended to be fun, exciting, and illuminating, not overwhelming or tedious.) Then sort through your Tarot deck to find cards that you feel best represent the components. Select your cards one by one, recording each one beside the component on your list as you go. You can choose your cards based on gut feelings, emotional reactions to the card images, the resemblance of figures on cards to people or situations—whatever works for you. For example, if you were working with a memory of the first time you attended a circus, the lion on the Strength card might remind you of the female lion tamer who happened to throw you a rose after her performance. So you choose the Strength card to represent that particular moment from your experience.

The other way to choose cards is to hold the entire snapshot in your mind's eye instead of writing down its individual components. Then look through the Tarot deck and pick the cards that seem to "speak" to you about the situation in general. Set your chosen cards apart from the rest of the deck and record your reason—even if it is "just a feeling"—for selecting each one. My husband, Ron, prefers to use this method when creating his BIT Snapshots; he forgoes writing down the actual components but holds the memory, movie, or situation in his mind's eye as he's looking through a Tarot deck. In one instance, he created a BIT Snapshot of a pivotal day when he and I, just friends at the time, connected deeply at a golf outing. That event signaled the rapid evolution from us being "just friends" to something else. The day before the outing, Ron's dad had written him an enigmatic note saying, "Look for her, son. She's there." As my husband went through the Tarot to capture the event in a BIT Snapshot, he chose the King of Swords to represent his dad, because the man shown on this card of his Tarot deck physically resembled his father.

Your level of experience with the Tarot will likely determine how you select your corresponding cards. If you're familiar with all seventy-eight cards of the Tarot and already associate a certain meaning with each card, you might find that a particular card automatically springs to mind for each element. Then again, it may not. You may find yourself shuffling through your deck and coming across a card that may not be one that you thought you'd choose for a particular component, but which seems like the perfect fit because of some type of unconscious personal association. That's the beauty of the BIT Method—it prompts you to unearth associations from the unconscious and bring them into the light of your conscious mind. (For this reason, the BIT Method works especially well for decoding puzzling dreams.)

Because I've studied and used the Tarot for years, I have dozens of associations stored in my particular "Fool's pouch." While I often dig around in there when doing readings or contemplating the Tarot, I remain open to intuition for fresh interpretations or use the BIT Method to generate new ones.

## A Sample BIT Snapshot

I'm going to walk you through the creation of a BIT Snapshot to give you an idea of how *I* often perform the BIT Method.

Recently, my husband and I took our son to see a live Sesame Street production. We also did other things throughout the day. Here are a few components of the day that I zeroed in on to create my BIT Snapshot: buying the production tickets online, going to the actual show, going to a restaurant afterward, and going to Wal-Mart. (Of course, I could have chosen the characters from the show, the meal itself, or even the drive home to pair with Tarot cards.) What follows is a BIT Snapshot, showing the components I chose and explanations on the Tarot card selections. For this BIT Snapshot, I used the *Pictorial Key Tarot* by Davide Corsi.

***Buying Tickets,* Six of Pentacles:** In many decks, the Six of Pentacles shows a figure giving coins to individuals. Some artists portray the giver as a wealthy man holding a scale and the receivers as mendicants on the street. Based on imagery alone, there is some exchange of money or goods implied for the Six of Pentacles. Some of the personal associations I have for this card are based on motifs of giving and receiving, including going into debt, "robbing Peter to pay Paul," charity work, donations, receiving help in a time of need, obtaining loans, and so on. I also associate this card with buying on credit or with credit cards in general. Because I ordered the tickets online,

I had to use a credit card. Therefore, the Six of Pentacles came to mind when I was thinking of the actual purchase.

If I had chosen to represent myself in this component rather than the transaction, I would have selected the Queen of Pentacles. In this card from the *Pictorial Key Tarot*, a green-clad queen gazes at a large gold coin before her. Just as the queen ponders the coin before her, I did take a few moments to consider if the show was worth the money, especially since we had taken my son to see a different live show two months prior.

*The Show,* **Six of Cups:** My husband noted that perhaps my son was getting a little too old for kiddie-oriented live shows. He had no more than uttered that phrase when, on noticing the smirk on my face, he commented wryly, "You do this as much—or more—for yourself, don't you?" I burst out laughing. Of course I do! I grew up on *Sesame Street*, so seeing a live show with Bert, Ernie, Elmo, Cookie Monster, Big Bird, Grover, the Count, and Oscar filled me with glee. Many Tarotists associate the Six of Cups with nostalgia, despite the fact that in many Rider-Waite–style decks, the card image alone lacks any indication of this meaning (only showing a figure presenting a flower-filled cup to a child). Nostalgia is one possible meaning that I, too, have used for this card. Although a few cards could have adequately captured other aspects of the show—including my son's delight and an unexpected show-ender that scared the bejeezus out of us (canisters of confetti exploded out into the audience and a lid hit my husband in the head)—I chose the Six of Cups because the show stirred thirty-year-old nostalgic memories within me.

*The Restaurant,* **Three of Pentacles:** In the *Pictorial Key Tarot*, a figure wearing an apron holds a group of paintbrushes in one hand and a palette in the other. He is standing inside a building with stone archways, presumably a church. Two men stand before him, one wearing a black robe with a gold cross necklace and the other wearing a rust-colored robe. These two men may very well be a priest and a monk who have commissioned a painter for work or who are at least supervising him. The monk gestures to the painter, perhaps giving him instructions.

Over time, some of the associations I've made for the Three of Pentacles include collaboration, commissioned work, employer/employee relations, architects, lay ministry, home remodeling, service industries, and redecoration.

I chose this card to represent the restaurant because not only had the restaurant been refurbished since we'd last been there, but there was also a completely different atmosphere. In place of the once consistently enthusiastic, competent young wait staff in a noisy, crowded dining room, now there were bored-looking youth milling near the front of the restaurant, decorations that bore tacky price tags to indicate that the items were for sale, and only a few diners. While five waitresses stood at the front talking—and often looking back at our table—we waited for over ten minutes before a server even came up to take our order for drinks!

The food was good, as always, but the vibe, décor, and service were dismal. It's uncertain if the changes were the result of new management or something else. I chose the Three of Pentacles because this card implies some kind of management/worker interactions, from my perspective. And, because I associate the pentacles/earth suit with the physical world—including hunger, eating, food, buildings, material goods, health, and money—this card reminded me (food quality aside) of the disappointing changes in the restaurant, especially the poor service and changes in the dining-room arrangement and gift-shop products.

*Going to Wal-Mart,* **Seven of Pentacles** and **Seven of Cups:** In a talk with my intrepid editor one Friday night, she advised me to get either a flash drive or some rewritable CDs to back up my work. (Yes, you read right: until then, I did not back up my work as I was working on a project!) My main reason for going to the mega store was to get a flash drive so I had a way to back up my files.

In the Seven of Pentacles from the *Pictorial Key Tarot*, a figure holds a rake in one hand, and the other hand is on his hip. He is gazing at a large tree before him, which is laden with seven gold coins. One of the associations I've made for this card is evaluating work or investment, pruning, choosing whether to continue with a present course, and so on. Consistent with my own associations with the number seven in numerology (which happens to be my life path number), I see all the sevens in the Minor Arcana as indicating some kind of deliberation, evaluation, or strategic action. Because I was in the editing process for this book, I was indeed evaluating my work (as was my editor!) and making necessary changes. Not only that, but I was also making a strategic decision to invest in a potentially timesaving, manuscript-preserving purchase like a flash drive.

While the Seven of Pentacles is a fine card by itself to represent the trip to Wal-Mart, I just had to pick the Seven of Cups as well. A figure stands before seven golden chalices, each laden with different items—a castle, a laurel wreath, sparkling jewels, a dragon, and so on. I often associate this card with indecision or being confronted with many options. And, to tell you the truth, almost every time I go into a Wal-Mart, the dizzying array of choices numbs my brain and drains my energy. I definitely get good buys there, but I do pay a price for it (and not just in the wallet).

These are just a small sampling of components and possible card choices to give you a feel for how simple yet thought-provoking the BIT Method can be. By trying your hand at re-creating any scenario—real or fictitious, personal or from the world's stage—you keep adding to the pouch of meanings that can serve you in your future use of the Tarot.

Even if you're a seasoned Tarot user, I also suggest actually laying out the cards you've chosen, because I guarantee that the visual line of pictures will give you additional insights. When doing the BIT Method, I often lay out the selected cards in a row and "read" the story I've created, as depicted in the card imagery. I'm always amazed at the additional, often surprising revelations that pop out as I gaze at the line of cards.

For example, as I was gazing at the line of cards from my sample BIT Snapshot, I noticed that the figure in the Six of Cups is standing at the left of the card and pointing rightward, while the monk in the Three of Pentacles is standing on the right side of the card and pointing leftward. I recalled that in handwriting analysis (one of my hobbies), left to right indicates past to future. While I was indeed nostalgic for the *Sesame Street* characters of my past, I was able to share them with my son in the present, and we have a shared experience we'll carry into the future as a fond memory. With the Three of Pentacles, my husband and I were looking to the past when ruing the decline of a good restaurant (although we did try to make the best of it).

Over time, you may find that your final BIT Snapshots aren't as cemented as you thought, especially as your perspective shifts or as you mature as a person. For example, you may have once considered an event heartbreaking or overwhelming, but after doing the BIT Method and seeing what cards you paired with it, you realize that you now see it as an incredible learning experience or even a gift. When your perspective shifts, the cards you select will likely change as well. In fact, you may want to revisit your BIT Snapshots after a time to see if and how your card selections change.

To get the most out of the BIT Method, I recommend that you record in your notebook the components of your mental picture, the cards you chose for each element, and your reasons for those choices. In addition, recording your answers to the questions in the "Your Turn" exercises at the end of each BIT Snapshot story will ensure that you retain your associations, plus give you something to refer to over and over again. I think you'll find that the reasons *why* you select particular cards (and why you left out certain ones) will reveal insights about your thoughts, feelings, attitudes, and worldview, which can be extraordinarily enlightening and therapeutic.

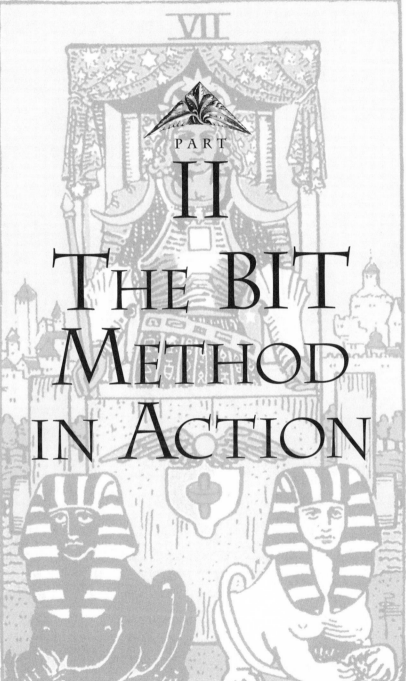

PART

# II
# THE BIT
# METHOD
# IN ACTION

THE CHARIOT.

**THE HIGH PRIESTESS.**

# *Personal Experiences*

## FINDING MY WAY BACK TO FAITH

*Mark McElroy*

After years of not being involved in religion at all (when I left fundamentalism, I tossed the faith-baby out with the bath water), I found myself involved in a loving, accepting community at Saint Mark United Methodist Church in Atlanta. This was a massively transformational moment for me because, in leaving the church the first time, I'd isolated myself from roles that had always been a huge part of my life, including those of teacher and leader. At Saint Mark, I found my way back to a community of faith where I could lead classes, contribute to a greater good, and still be accepted for who I really am.

Decks used: *Rider-Waite Tarot, Lo Scarabeo Tarot* (designed by Mark), *Tarot of Dreams, Thoth Tarot,* and *Bright Idea Deck* (also designed by Mark).

**The Fool** (from the *Rider-Waite Tarot*): This card, showing a young man standing at the edge of a cliff as if about to step off it, illustrates taking a leap of faith. When I set out to find a church to attend in Atlanta, I had no idea what I would encounter. I knew, though, that a part of me needed to return to church, so I took the plunge. (I bounced off the edge of the cliff a couple of times—finding churches that didn't quite fit—before finding Saint Mark.)

**The Hierophant** (from the *Rider-Waite Tarot* and *Lo Scarabeo Tarot*): This card (at least as it appears in the Rider-Waite and certainly as I designed it and artist Anna Lazzarini illustrated it for the *Lo Scarabeo Tarot*) embodies everything I *don't* want my faith to be: a mask, a rigid structure, an unquestioning obedience to authority—structured, "high church" religion.

**Faith (traditionally titled the Hierophant)** (from the *Tarot of Dreams*): This card, simply titled Faith in this deck, depicts an older man bowing his head in prayer while encircled by nine symbols from various spiritual traditions. The imagery really resonated with my new approach to a connection with God. I was being drawn to something simple, organic, and older than I. For me, the personal, mystical experience—the internal transformation that faith can achieve—is much more important than the name tacked up over the door of the building.

**The Chariot** (from the *Rider-Waite Tarot*): It was time for a change. My faithless path had taken me as far as I could go. I needed to break down my own hesitations and limitations, and move confidently forward on my quest to rediscover my own, adult faith.

**Judgement** (from the *Rider-Waite Tarot*): This old card, with its classic image of the fundamentalist Day of Judgement, represents the energy and fear that, for two decades, were the engine that governed my faith. I used to have nightmares about the Rapture: hearing that terrible trumpet, watching everyone but me rise up into the sky, and jumping up and down in a vain effort to join them.

**The World** (from the *Rider-Waite Tarot*): The iconography of this card—with the Four Evangelists in the four corners, the almond-shaped mandorla (wreath) surrounding the dancing figure in the center—is familiar to anyone who has studied classical or European Christian iconography. The figure in the center of more traditional versions is the transformed Christ; in some very old decks, this card shows the New Jerusalem, complete with a white city coming down from the sky. To me, the card represents my joy over finding a transformative new faith—the true church, stripped of the fearful trappings of Judgement and the harsh sermons of the Hierophant.

**Ace of Cups** (from the *Rider-Waite Tarot*): The first time I took communion at Saint Mark, I burst into tears. Why did I ever believe, even for a moment, that men and their prejudices could have the power to bar me from God's table? In that instant, my perception of my relationship with God was changed forever.

**Two of Cups** (from the *Rider-Waite Tarot*): Sharing this experience with my partner, Clyde, made it even richer. For him, our return to church meant a reconnection with the church of his childhood. While at Saint Mark, we also became leaders of the Couple's Class, a Sunday School class designed to honor and support couples, people hoping to find a partner, or people who had been in a couple and who, someday, hoped to be in a couple again. Our participation in that class literally changed our lives.

**Six of Pentacles** (from the *Lo Scarabeo Tarot*): Working with the church took us outside ourselves and got us working for the community again. Working with the Breakfast Club, serving breakfast to Atlanta's homeless, involved us with a meaningful service project and helped us appreciate our own blessings all the more.

**Science (traditionally titled the Six of Swords)** (from the *Thoth Tarot* and *Bright Idea Deck*): Titled Science in the *Thoth Tarot* and *Bright Idea Deck*, this card, for me, has always been about ways of knowing. For years, I had depended on strict humanism as a way of approaching the world, and, frankly, that approach didn't offer the fulfillment I craved. In the end, there are many ways of knowing, and the mystical path I'm on is much more rewarding than the pretense of total objectivity ever was.

**Ace of Wands** (from the *Lo Scarabeo Tarot*): Always a card about taking the reins and making your will manifest in reality, this card captures my strong, sincere desire to be closer to God and the burning need I felt to take action to reconnect with a faith that made sense to me and helped me make a difference in the lives of others.

## COMMENTARY

In Mark's re-creation using the BIT Method, he chose cards from several decks, including the *Lo Scarabeo Tarot* that he designed, to represent his experience. If you own several decks or can recall images from more than one deck, your reservoir of possible cards for selection expands exponentially, but using multiple decks is by no means required.

Interestingly, Mark chose the same card, the Hierophant, from two different decks to represent two distinct versions of religion. The papal figure in full regalia sitting before two bowing monks in the Rider-Waite image implied formality and blind obeisance to external religious authority, while the same card in the *Tarot of Dreams*, renamed Faith, represented to Mark a personal, mystical spiritual experience generated from the inside.

In his *Bright Idea Deck* (illustrated by Eric Hotz), Mark renamed the Chariot card Advancement. The Chariot card often indicates shattering limitations and overcoming obstacles, a meaning usually depicted by an ancient vehicle pulled by two horses. The Bright Idea version shows a modern, fresh interpretation of this image: a man busting through a white picket fence on a Segway.

In the Rider-Waite image, the Ace of Cups shows a dove descending from above and carrying in its mouth a wafer bearing the emblem of a cross. The overflowing cup below the bird is embossed with an upside-down M, which, according to Robert Place, author of *The Tarot: History, Symbolism, and Divination*, associates the cup with Mary, the mother of Jesus. In the New Testament, the white dove is associated with the Holy Spirit, and, in some religious traditions, the wafer represents the communion Eucharist, considered to be the body of Christ through transubstantiation. All of these associations make the Ace of Cups a logical card to connect with Holy Communion, as Mark did. Because of its religious symbolism, I tend to see the Ace of Cups as personal, direct communion with the Divine. The water from the cup can be seen as symbolizing a release of emotions, including relief or ecstatic joy—emotions Mark exhibited during the act of taking communion.

In the Two of Cups from the *Rider-Waite Tarot* and *Lo Scarabeo Tarot*, a couple holding cups reach toward one another. The Two of Cups is often interpreted as sharing and intimacy, especially since the number two often indicates joining or couplehood and the suit of cups represents feelings. Mark understandably chose this card to symbolize the emotional and spiritual experience he had shared with his partner.

The *Lo Scarabeo Tarot*'s Six of Pentacles depicts a human hand filled with coins at the top of the card and another hand at the bottom—empty, and perhaps hoping or expecting to receive some of those coins. As I noted in my sample BIT Snapshot in chapter 2, this image is often associated with charity work. So it is logical that Mark chose it to represent the community-outreach activities he became involved with through his church.

The *Thoth Tarot* deck, designed by Aleister Crowley and painted with stunning sacred geometrical strokes by Frieda Harris, is a challenging esoteric deck for many. The Minor Arcana, while attractively illustrated, doesn't depict action scenes like the Rider-Waite decks. Instead, keywords based on Crowley's *Book of Thoth* give a form of shorthand to the card meanings. As Mark pointed out, the Six of Swords is dubbed Science in both the *Thoth Tarot* and the *Bright Idea Deck*. In his *Creative*

*Brainstorming with the Bright Idea Deck* companion book, Mark notes that card Yellow 6/Science indicates "abandoning approaches that have been proven outdated or problematic."

Explaining the scientific connection to the Six of Swords, a card astrologically associated with Mercury in Aquarius, *Thoth Tarot* expert Lon Milo DuQuette observes in his book *Understanding Aleister Crowley's Thoth Tarot*, "Someone with Mercury in Aquarius in his or her natal horoscope is said to have a keen, analytical mind and an extraordinary ability to concentrate. He or she is also intensely curious and enjoys examining both sides of a question. Sounds like a scientist, doesn't it?"

In Rider-Waite decks, the Ace of Wands is a budding branch held by a hand emerging from a white cloud. In the *Lo Scarabeo Tarot*, this card has a more fiery connotation as swirling clouds of red and orange surround the singular wand. The wands suit is considered masculine for its outward, action-oriented focus, and the wand is often considered a phallic symbol— further connecting it to masculine, or yang, energy. Mark's application of the Ace of Wands is quite personal. I would not have associated this card with a "strong, sincere desire to be closer to God and the burning need . . . to take action to reconnect with a faith that made sense to me." But that's the beauty of the BIT Method—it allows you to discover your own, unique interpretations of the cards.

## YOUR TURN

— Think of your own views on religion and spirituality. Which cards would *you* choose to represent religion or a spiritual experience? What about your view of God?

— Have you ever witnessed someone having a "religious experience"? Have you ever attended a ceremony in a church, such as a baptism, christening, first communion, wedding, bar/bat mitzvah, or ordination? What cards would you select to represent the surroundings, those involved, or the general mood?

— Recall a historical or current event involving religion or religious figures. Which cards would you select to represent the people involved and the ideology of the participants?

# DISCOVERING THE TAROT
### Mary K. Greer

On Christmas in 1968, I went to the house of my best friend, Nancy, so we could show each other our presents. A distant relative had sent her a book (Eden Gray's *Tarot Revealed*) about strange fortune-telling cards but no deck. I was jealous that she had access to this book filled with mysterious images and scenes that could somehow tell us all about ourselves. I decided I had to find the cards, so I began asking everyone where to go. Finally, someone told me about this strange metaphysical bookstore on the other side of Tampa.

Borrowing my brother's car (it had a hole in the floor and had to be double clutched), I set out on what felt like a quest for a treasure. At the bookstore, I bought a University Books Waite deck and discovered the whole world of "occult metaphysics."

At the time, I was an English major with a theater minor, studying Greek myth, Joseph Campbell's hero's journey, Carl Jung's concept of individuation and archetypes, and, soon after, Fritz Perls's Gestalt therapy. I recognized all of these in the Tarot. For me, the cards represented a way to use symbols to see the real drives and motivations of people rather than accurately predict events or tell people what to do.

Deck used: *Rider-Waite Tarot*

**Ten of Pentacles:** With its images of a couple, children, and a pair of dogs, this card depicts the sense of a family home at Christmas. To me, it also includes the element of the intriguing gift from a near stranger; like the child shown sneaking a peek at the magically robed outsider, the Tarot seemed to provide an opening into a world beyond my normal one.

**Two of Cups:** This was the closest I could come to a card for my friend, Nancy. At the time, we shared so much, including an interest in literature and theater. It felt like this particular season of our relationship was an opportunity for both of us to explore something powerful and strange. In actuality, it marked the beginning of a divergence of our paths and interests.

**Seven of Cups:** Whereas the occult scared Nancy, it intrigued me and set off a deep longing to know more. I wasn't sure where all of this metaphysical investigation would take me, but within that first year of exploring the Tarot, I decided that one day I would write a book about the Tarot and that I had to teach it as an academic course in college. Now the questions were how to gain all the knowledge and experience I would need and what would be helpful and what dangerous.

**The Chariot:** Considering the condition of the car I borrowed, I thought about making this card, often associated with vehicles, the Chariot reversed, but I safely made the journey and achieved my goal. In fact, it was the first time I recognized what became a familiar scenario. I was on what I came to call one of my quests, an active search for something magical and mysterious.

**The Moon:** This card represents the realm into which I was now moving. When I was a child, my family moved frequently. I would always go to the library at our new location to look up three words in the card catalog: *gypsy*, *witch*, and *magic*. All I ever found were books on hauntings and stuffy tomes on yoga. When I saw that book on Tarot that Christmas, I had an intimation that I had found what I'd always been looking for. That metaphysical bookstore then opened my eyes to the many facets of the occult. To me, the Moon card is also the Jungian world of archetypes, symbols, and the unconscious that I immediately recognized in the Tarot.

**The Hermit:** With a figure holding a lantern to light the way, this card represents me as a seeker through the landscape of the occult and the Tarot. I would have loved to find a teacher, but all my early studies were on my own. It was at least seven years before I had the opportunity to discuss and learn from someone who knew more about Tarot than I did. Only years later did I discover that my lifetime cards (based on my birthday) were the Moon and the Hermit (who walks the Moon's path up to the mountaintop).

**Seven of Pentacles:** This card was my everyday reality of my Tarot studies: learning piece by piece. I gathered and worked on text after text, and I perfected my reading skills through trial and error. I made slow, steady, sustained progress, year by year, accumulating knowledge and experiences.

**Six of Cups:** While the study of Tarot was a lonely process, right from the beginning I discovered the amazingly deep and sincere connection to another person that was possible during a Tarot reading. This profound yet simple gift was one I could offer and share with others, heart-to-heart, to take us past dissembling to a place of truth and innocence.

**Judgement:** In looking back on this episode, I see it as a major crossroads or turning point in my life where I was called to my life's work. I heard the call and responded, and, in doing so, I emerged from a limited worldview into a much larger existence. Through Tarot, I found a way to communicate with Spirit and my higher self.

## COMMENTARY

In her book *Mary K. Greer's 21 Ways to Read a Tarot Card*, Mary notes that the Seven of Pentacles is astrologically correlated with Saturn in Taurus. Saturn is a planet of limitation, structure, and diligence, while Taurus is a fixed earth sign. The fixed signs of Taurus, Leo, Scorpio, and Aquarius are said to be stubborn and tenacious, so it makes sense that Mary associated this card with slow, steady, and sustained progress in her studies.

In the Rider-Waite deck, the Six of Cups card shows a figure giving a cup of flowers to a little girl. As a result, many Tarotists, including Mary, associate this card with simple or heartfelt gifts.

The Judgement card in the Rider-Waite deck shows an angel blowing a trumpet and several nude individuals standing below the angel, in boxes, arms raised. Although some translate the individuals as the Christian belief of resurrection on a final day of judgement (when "the last trump sounds"), the blast of the horn can also indicate a wake-up call, as well as hearing a call, as Mary has demonstrated in her BIT Snapshot.

## YOUR TURN

— Think of a time that felt mysterious or laden with secrets. Who or what was involved? Which cards remind you of the situation?

— Have you ever encountered someone who held beliefs different from yours or engaged in behavior that was quite different from your own? How would you re-create your thoughts and reactions using the Tarot?

— Think of a historical figure, famous person, or character that couldn't leave well enough alone. What do you suppose drove them, and where did their persistence and/or curiosity lead them? Select cards to represent the circumstances.

# YOU CAN CATCH A ROBIN IF YOU PUT SALT ON ITS TAIL

*Ann Cass*

When I was five years old (or thereabouts), I heard the phrase "You can catch a robin if you put salt on its tail." That sounded great to me, so I took one of my grandmother's saltshakers and walked out on a bright summer day to catch a robin. I got back about three hours later with an empty saltshaker, a bit of sunburn, and lots of near misses.

This was probably the point at which my grandmother decided that she needed somebody else to cope with me during the day, so she put me in a day school down the block. Or she might have simply told me that this phrase was a way of saying a person *couldn't* catch a robin. (That part isn't as clear in my memory as my stalking robins across the lawns of all the neighbors.) Whatever she did, I suspect that if she hadn't done something, I would have refilled the saltshaker and gone back out yet again.

The rational side of me knows that this phrase is only a way of saying that you can't catch a robin. But to this day, I think that part of me believes that if I'd only kept going, I might have done it. I got so close so many times!

Deck used: *WorldTree Tarot* (designed by Ann)

**Page of Pentacles:** For me, this is a card of childhood wonder. It's a big world, and *anything* might be out there (with a positive slant on *anything*).

**Page of Cups:** Questing on dolphinback—that's my version of this card in the *WorldTree Tarot*. I suspect that somewhere in my mind was the idea that if I caught a robin, it would have to be a magical bird that would take me on an adventure. I started reading at about age three, and by the time I was about five, I'd gone through a huge collection of fairy tales, as well as the original *Tarzan of the Apes*. I can't remember having any problem with the possibility that animals could talk. So I was looking for a beginning to something I couldn't even imagine, rather than just trying to catch a robin.

**Seven of Swords:** I chose this card to represent the robin—the trickster who walks off with your stuff. The same card in the *Ferret Tarot* deck is even better, because the ferret is blowing a taunting razzberry at you while he does it!

**King of Wands:** The saltshaker as a tool of transformation. If someone had told me I had to have a magical tool to catch a robin, I probably wouldn't have bothered. But a plain, mundane saltshaker? That *was* a magical tool at the time. (Janet's note: In the companion booklet to the *WorldTree Tarot*, Ann says that the inspiration for the King of Wands card likely came from the description of Coyote's magic mirror in the book *Changer's Moon*, by Jo Clayton. Ann notes that this card represents "a gateway for all the realities that are, or may be," which is, indeed, what the saltshaker symbolized to her as a young girl with dreams of adventure. In her version of this card, the King of Wands sits under the open sky holding a crystal-tipped wand. He seems to be gazing at a window-like portal that extends upward from the ground, reflecting images of lush, vibrant foliage and landscapes.)

**The Moon:** This card is about dreams and their reflections in reality. You can catch a moonbeam in your hand—*if* you're willing to cup a handful of the water to catch its reflection. The moon in your hand, however, is going to be smaller, with wiggly edges, compared to the luster of the original moon.

NOTE FROM ANN: Janet's BIT Method is an awe-inspiring process even if you really know your own deck or know more than one deck well enough to make connections. After the first two or three card possibilities came up in my mind, I got my WorldTree deck and started going through it card by card. I had to take a strong hold of myself because there were at least twenty cards that popped up and started showing me meanings connected with my uncaught robin. Then I went back through the situation again, looking for different aspects (like the saltshaker) that I wouldn't normally try to designate with a card, and found even more enlightening insights coming up. Wow!

## COMMENTARY

Ann's note shows how powerful the BIT Method can be even for Tarot authors and deck creators who know the cards inside and out. There are literally thousands of facets to the Tarot, and every time you examine a memory, current event, story, or movie with the BIT Method, another symbol, correlation, or insight becomes illuminated. And as you change, your personal "stories" change—and thus the Tarot changes with you. Ann's brightly colored, computer-generated *WorldTree Tarot* deck is inspired by the Rider-Waite, but its unusual patterns, crystalline figures, and vibrant hues make it quite distinct. The WorldTree Page of Pentacles shows an opened-armed youth gazing at what looks to be a large orb, perhaps a planet or our own world. Many Tarotists associate the pages with actual children, especially since in so many renderings the pages do indeed look quite young. In addition, some Tarotists see pages as youthful approaches to their respective suits or even beginnings in general.

For example, Ann's imagery of the Page of Pentacles seems to depict a child in awe of something bigger than him- or herself. It makes sense that the youth of the page combined with the earthly suit of pentacles would indicate childlike wonder, especially in terms of the physical world. This connection reminds me of how when we are children, everything seems bigger, larger than life. For example, a hill that seemed so daunting when we went sledding as children looks like a mere bump when we see it as an adult. Or a stately tree oft climbed that seemed like it would touch the sky seems rather tame when we are "grown up." But the energy of a page card can even apply to an adult: if we remain open to new things and perhaps recapture (or re-create) a sense of childlike curiosity, we become pagelike in our attitude and experience.

In the spirit of the Rider-Waite, Ann depicts the Seven of Swords as a figure looking over his shoulder as he walks away with an armload of swords. Because he looks as if he's tiptoeing away stealthily, some Tarotists associate this card with theft. As Ann describes, however, this card from the *Ferret Tarot* is more mischievous and elusive rather than malicious.

Ann's Moon card, like many in the Rider-Waite tradition, shows a body of water. In the case of the WorldTree rendering, a crescent moon sits in an open sky at dusk above a river valley. Many Tarotists associate the Moon with actual night dreams, as well as daydreams. There's quite a bit of mythology surrounding the moon, especially its association with werewolves, strange antics during the full moon, and madness in general. (After all, the word "lunar" is derived from the same root as "lunatic.") Just as rippled reflections in the water distort reality, the Moon card can reflect some type of imitation of what appears to be solid, perhaps even projecting a mirage-like illusion. As a result, some Tarotists associate the Moon with deception.

## YOUR TURN

— When you were a child, did you believe you could accomplish something magical, or perhaps feel that you could access a gateway to adventure if you could somehow encounter a larger-than-life character, an unusual object, or even a mythological creature? Choose cards to represent your feelings, expectations, and assumptions, as well as the source of the "magic" and how your perspective changed (or remained the same) as you got older.

— Recall a situation where someone you knew settled for "the next best thing," when he or she "reached for the Moon" by only observing its reflection in a handful of water. For example, if an individual can't afford a trip to Hawaii, he or she may settle for looking at a travel book filled with pictures. A family without room in their home for a seven-foot Christmas tree may settle for a tabletop tree, a wreath, or an evergreen swag. Which cards seem to represent the situation?

— Recall a movie, novel, or fairy tale where an individual used or sought a special talisman, key, text, remedy, or secret. Which cards would you choose to symbolize the main characters, obstacles, helpers, and eventual outcome?

# THE CRACKED SPRING
## Janet Boyer

My husband, Ron, worked half a day one Saturday since he had an appointment to take our car for its yearly inspection. Later, we sat at the table in our backyard and talked about our day. I happened to have the Universal Waite deck with me and used the opportunity to take a BIT Snapshot of his day and re-create it with the Tarot. I went through the deck, picking out cards that seemed to jump out at me as I thought about what we shared. Interestingly, after I quickly picked several cards and explained my selections to Ron, he pointed out additional insights that correlated with his experience.

Deck used: *Universal Waite Tarot*

**The Sun:** I picked this card for obvious reasons: the day was gorgeous, one of the first springlike days we'd had in a while. There wasn't a cloud in the sky; the sun was bright and warm—perfect. The sunflowers in this card reminded me of the yellow dandelions dotting our yard that seemed to have sprouted overnight.

**Eight of Pentacles:** Ron works at a local factory as a radio-frequency technician. He welds cleats onto conveyor-type belts using high-frequency waves, and these belts are used by companies all over the world. His work creating custom belts for clients is quite specialized, requiring innovation and attention to detail. I chose the Eight of Pentacles because it shows an artisan at his workbench, hammering details onto a golden disc, dedicated to doing the best job he possibly can.

**The Chariot:** When I think of the Chariot in literal terms, I usually think "car."

**Seven of Pentacles:** A man standing in a field leans on a shovel or hoe, looking at a bush sprouting six pentacles. One coin lies on the ground. When I saw this card, the man seemed to be inspecting the bush, contemplating if it was up to his standards. I chose this card to represent the man who actually performed the car inspection. He told Ron that one of the coil springs in the rear was cracked, and the mechanic recommended that both springs be replaced, at a cost of $300 or more. Our car wouldn't pass inspection without the repairs, and, if the spring snapped, it could possibly puncture a tire.

As I looked at the Seven of Pentacles, I realized that the pentacle on the ground seemed to have fallen off the bush, which represented to me the broken car part that needed fixing. Although the rest of the car was in great shape (the six pentacles still on the bush), the mechanic had to focus on the fallen "pentacle" for our safety.

**Two of Pentacles:** A figure juggles two coins, and there is a green infinity "belt" that seems to surround the coins. In the background, two ships sail on tumultuous waves. I chose this card because the figure seemed to be juggling the coins, which made me think of juggling finances. Ron and I had to figure out when to schedule the appointment for the repairs based on our current financial situation. This card represented our debate about the when and how of paying for this repair.

Ron pointed out that there were two coins in the card—and two springs needed to be replaced. The mechanic noted that if only one of the springs were replaced, the car would be off kilter. The figure in the Two of Pentacles seems to be balancing his coins quite admirably, even as he stands on one foot; replacing both springs would literally keep our car in balance.

**Four of Pentacles:** A seated figure holds one coin tightly to his chest; two are firmly under his feet, and another sits atop his head. I chose this card because the unexpected repair would make finances tight until our next payday, and I knew we'd have to watch our money closely.

Ron observed that the man's back was to numerous buildings in the background, which looked like a populated area. Ron commented that it was as if the man had to turn his back on the city. To us, the city represents shopping and dining out, and since we live in a rural area, the city is miles away from our home. As a result, it was important for us to stay close to home until the springs were fixed, for safety's sake. Noting the coin on the card figure's head, Ron mentioned that he had to use his head with the coin (finances)—something that we would, indeed, need to do in terms of budgeting.

**Nine of Cups:** Ron happened to bring an assortment of snacks and a cold drink to the table, so as we shared the events of the day, he was munching rather happily. I felt this card, which shows a smiling man seated in the foreground with a cup-lined table behind him, aptly represented my snacking husband.

**Ten of Cups:** As I was selecting cards to represent Ron's experience, our son, Noah, came out to the backyard and began chattering away, frolicking in the warm sun and pretending to be an astronaut on the moon. Meanwhile, Ron recounted some hilarious pictures he saw at work called "Porn for Women," which depicted one man vacuuming and another offering a large piece of chocolate cake to a woman, saying, "Here, eat this. It pains me to see you so thin." (I laughed so hard I almost fell off my chair!)

I couldn't help but think of the Ten of Cups, which shows a couple with arms outstretched, a rainbow of cups above them with two children playing to the side. There is a decidedly rural scene in the background, including a stream. And it just so happens that after a downpour of rain, we have a small creek running behind our house.

## COMMENTARY

Before re-creating this particular situation using the BIT Method, I wouldn't have associated the Seven of Pentacles with an inspector. Now, I can add "car inspector" or "mechanic" to my cache of associations with that card. In fact, I can now see how the Seven of Pentacles could represent any type of individual who evaluates something for the express purpose of pointing out something awry in the material world—including finances, possessions, property, or even the body. I then began thinking of other such diagnosticians, including auditors, insurance adjusters, evaluators, and home inspectors. Even appraisers could be connected to the Seven of Pentacles.

## YOUR TURN

— When have you ever been evaluated in some way or had something appraised or diagnosed? Select appropriate cards to represent your experience.

— Think of a time when you were a bystander to an event involving cars or other vehicles. Re-create what you saw, smelled, heard, and so on with cards that remind you of these things.

— Recall a historical event involving a car or cars, or perhaps a movie, book, TV show, or commercial where a car figures prominently in the theme. Which cards would correspond to what you read or saw?

# Overcoming Writer's/Artist's Block
### *Lisa Hunt*

Have you ever felt tired and depleted after tackling a monumental task? There are the initial feelings of euphoria for a job (hopefully) well done, but then it's time to get back to work. What do you do if you simply can't restart your engines and find yourself procrastinating instead?

The intensity of my work requires that I wash off my palette, so to speak, and refill the well before embarking on another cycle of creative activity. When it's time to sit my butt back down and relaunch the creative thinking process, it is not always easy. Sure, the peripheral stuff like sketching, note taking, and research remain fixed parts of my daily routine, but the more demanding aspects of writing or drawing finished material under deadline is a whole 'nother ball of wax! The carefree repose of doodle time must give way to thoughtful compositions. Having just experienced one of these transitions, I felt this would be a great time to demonstrate the effective nature of Janet's BIT Method when confronting writer's/artist's block (or any situation that has you feeling stuck).

Deck used: *Fantastical Creatures Tarot* (illustrated by Lisa)

**Seven of Swords:** Ah yes, time to get back to work! I have all my notes collated, my research organized, and the material rehearsed in my head. The muses are beckoning me back to the pleasurable realm of creativity, but my mind is playing games with me—finding more excuses for procrastinating. The Seven of Swords exemplifies the conflicts that I'm experiencing between latent thought processes and a proactive response. I need to get past the debris that is clouding up my sensibilities.

**Ten of Wands:** The more I think about the necessity of beginning (not to mention the deadline), the more overwhelmed I become. I look at the piles of research with a sort of anxious enthusiasm. Where to begin? How can I get past the feelings of being overwhelmed by all that I *have* to do and just start doing it?

**The Hanged Man:** Medusa is looking me straight in the eyes with her cold, unflinching stare. She's thinking, "You're not getting past me!" I feel paralyzed in the grips of an intellectual stasis. I can't budge, and the clock isn't going to stand still while I get my act together. Where is that elusive inspiration that will propel me into another satisfying spate of creativity?

**The Hermit:** I back off. I decide I need to reflect some more. It is time to breathe, relax, and let go. I return to the books, write some more notes, and begin to consider the enticing nature of the next step. I attempt to unclutter the mind and let peace preside for the time being.

**The Moon:** Going a step further, I start digging deeper within. Searching for the epicenter of creative joy, I let my mind rest in the quietude of a more reflective part of my being. I come face to face with the very shadow that has erected the creative block in the first place and decide to confront it with calm confidence.

**Three of Wands:** Patience! By letting go of my anxieties, I move forward and start drafting a plan of action: *Okay now, this is what I want to accomplish today.* If I can break through that initial ice, I just know the muses will reign once again! Determined not to force anything, I sift through my pile of notes and let my eye gravitate to an aspect of my research that is particularly appealing at that moment in time. I pick up the folder and revisit the material. Why not give it a shot?

**Ace of Swords:** I sit down and write the first sentence, then the second, and then I lose count. It is as if the dam has finally broken. I feel a flood of images rolling through my brain with a thunderous assault. I just write and immerse myself in the pure joy of the process. Not only am I writing, but also I am sketching more ideas in between. Now the problem becomes how to channel all of this raw energy in a productive manner that maximizes the process.

**Knight of Cups:** Before long, I assume a good rhythm and am happy with the creative outflow as a result. I am no longer deliberating about what I *have* to do; instead, I'm thinking about all that I desire to do before I run out of hours that day. With my creative juices pumping at full force, I no longer view the deadline as an ominous oppressor.

**Eight of Pentacles:** A friend and fellow author once told me that she feels writers/artists have to go through an incubation period. We research, reflect, and when we start writing (or painting images), all of the material that was planted in the psyche becomes a crop ripe for harvest. The results are very satisfying. If there were no struggles along the way, the rewards would be less gratifying.

## COMMENTARY

Yet another benefit of creating BIT Snapshots is that the cards can illustrate *any* challenge or goal, providing a visual and conceptual roadmap that you can use when facing a similar situation in the future. By using a BIT Snapshot to capture how you navigated a particular challenge, you can use one or more cards—or the entire BIT Snapshot—as a talisman, visual affirmation, or symbolic map leading you to a specific goal. In fact, the little white book accompanying the *Fantastical Creatures Tarot* provides magickal uses for each card, which can encompass those intentions.

Lisa's *Fantastical Creatures Tarot* is a gorgeous deck that brims with a dizzying array of gods, goddesses, mythological creatures, and other stuff of legends. She and her cocreator, D. J. Conway, reinterpret the Tarot through the lens of cultural and literary mythos. For example, in mythology, the goddess Athena changed Medusa into a snake-haired monster whose deadly gaze turned humans into stone. The Hanged Man card often connotes suspension or waiting, so Lisa's interpretation of this card is aptly captured by the metaphorical "freeze" caused by Medusa's stare.

Although the actual cards of the *Fantastical Creatures Tarot* reflect traditional names (such as the Hanged Man, the Hermit, and Ten of Wands), the actual imagery is anything but traditional. The companion booklet explains the card images as well as its interpretation for the user. Although Lisa's paintings are based on a wide range of mythology, her Quick Reference Guide and D. J. Conway's booklet tie these images to widely accepted card meanings.

For example, the magical white unicorn represents the Moon card in this deck, while the Ace of Swords is Thor's Goats, the Ten of Wands is the Minotaur, the Three of Wands is the Djinn, and the Eight of Pentacles is Quetzalcoatl. Lisa's personal connections with the cards are also influenced, however, by some traditional meanings that she has come to associate with the cards: heavy burdens associated with the Ten of Wands, quiet retreat associated with the Hermit, reward for hard work with the Eight of Pentacles, powerful new mental energy with the Ace of Swords, patience and planning with the Three of Wands, and subconscious shadows and creative blocks with the Moon. But in the case of the Seven of Swords and Knight of Cups, she has an exceptionally original and personal take on these cards: mind games (even internal ones) for the former and deep involvement represented by the latter.

The Seven of Swords in the *Fantastical Creatures Tarot* swirls with energy as autumn leaves and swords surround a woman shape-shifting into a fox. This is one of the fox ladies of Asia, who are "tricky, ambiguous creatures, and masters of illusion," says the little white companion book to this deck. The book goes on to explain the divinatory meaning as "someone who doesn't reveal her/his true personality or plans."

The Celtic sea god Manannan Mac Lir represents the Knight of Cups in this deck. Also a shape-shifter, his magical protective armor rendered him invisible. According to the little white book, "When Manannan rode through the ocean waves, his vessel was powered only by the energy of the sea itself." Just as this sea god from the Celtic pantheon found propulsion in the powerful waves, Lisa found a creative rhythm that thrust her forward toward her deadline.

The Hermit from the *Fantastical Creatures Tarot* peeks from behind a flowering elder tree. This is the Old Lady of the Elder, who D. J. Conway notes is a "solitary creature, using the silent, reflective time" to nurture herself spiritually. Interestingly, Lisa had her mom model for this lovely card image.

## YOUR TURN

— Consider a time when you were at point A of a project or circumstance, but you longed to get to Z. Select cards to represent your thoughts, feelings, and actions along the way.

— Think of a surprising event when a person, team, or animal surmounted an incredible challenge. Illustrate what happened using the cards of your choice.

— Recall a famous artist, writer, or musician. Which cards would you pick to represent their style, impact, and body of work?

## JOURNEY THROUGH THE
## DARK NIGHT OF THE MIND

*Teresa Michelsen*

Our family has hereditary migraines. They usually start when someone is about age twenty, worsen when the person is between the ages of thirty and fifty or so, and then lessen somewhat after menopause. This story is about a journey that started when a migraine I had became permanent. It's called an intractable migraine, and that's a good name for it. I've lived with it ever since and have learned to manage it through a combination of techniques. It's changed my life in various ways, both difficult and positive. Among other things, I renewed my deep appreciation for Tarot through it.

Deck used: No particular deck, except for the Six of Swords from both the *Robin Wood Tarot* and the *Thoth Tarot*

**Nine of Swords:** The Nine of Swords, which usually shows a woman sitting up in bed, head held in her hands and a row of swords on the wall behind her, is the card I most associate with migraines. In this case, the stabbing pain of swords in the head was all too real. Migraines also give you a hypersensitivity to noise and light and can make it hard to sleep—not to mention the worry they cause as you try to go about a busy life and get your normal things done with this hypersensitivity going on all the time. They can also create something that feels like an electrical storm in your head and, for some people, cognitive-verbal dissociations and visual auras. All of these effects seem to fit with the swords suit and the abundance or over-stimulation associated with the nine.

**Judgement:** I had started a consulting business and gone out on my own about six months prior to the start of my intractable migraine. The Tarot reading I'd done on this new venture had indicated that it would be very successful but so painful that it would be something like giving birth. I had no idea what that could possibly mean. But on Easter Sunday of the following year, I found out—that was the day I got a migraine, and it just never went away. I was about to start my own trial by fire.

**Four of Swords:** A period of enforced inactivity began; other than making visits to the neurologist, nutritionist, and other health-care practitioners, I did nothing. I had to retreat and tell my clients that I would be unable to travel. In truth, there was very little work I *could* do, and I was confined to home and bed a lot of the time. I felt trapped and still. I could not even read properly as my eyesight was obscured by migraine aura, and my computer time was limited. There was, however, a voluntary element to this self-imposed isolation; I was choosing to try a variety of alternative treatments, such as yoga, elimination diet, and just giving it time, prior to going on medication full time.

**The Moon:** In spite of limited computer time, I turned my attention back to Tarot with as much energy as I had. I joined online discussion groups, the American Tarot Association (ATA), designed a Web site, and began doing readings online. The computer was almost my only connection to other people. I called my Web site Tarot Moon in recognition of where I was in my journey. I felt as though I were wandering in the dark, not knowing if I would ever be able to work again, and trying to find a reason to live in the absence of religious or spiritual beliefs. I found my inspiration in Tarot and in literature, where the dark night of the soul is recognized. In these realms, even when hope cannot be felt, there is an ability to trust in the fundamental patterns of life, to believe that even this, too, will pass, and the Star can be found someday. Without this hope, I am not sure what meaning I would have been able to find.

**Six of Swords:** After the alternative treatments I tried were unsuccessful, my neurologist pointed out that with my family history and the hormonal basis of the migraines (the Moon again), it was unlikely that I could expect those approaches alone to work. It was time to follow the path my mother had eventually taken and devise a full-time treatment program. I chose the Six of Swords not only because the version from the *Robin Wood Tarot* represents a journey to a better life, but also because of its association with science in the *Thoth Tarot* and other decks. The treatment regimen focuses on balancing hormones, a Western medication that prevents seizures in the brain, and vitamin enhancement that has been shown in trials to reduce migraines. On top of that, there are various fallback treatments if the migraines manage to break through all these stabilizing influences. I'm still traveling with my swords, but they are better in hand, the neurological flows contained and organized.

**Seven of Pentacles:** Then came a period of hard work to try to rebuild my life. First, I focused on being able to work again, as working was crucial to my self-esteem and retaining my self-sufficiency over the long term. Lo and behold, my clients had not deserted me but welcomed me back to the community. Once I felt that daily life and work were possible and the medication dosages were properly adjusted, it was time to lose the weight I had gained during almost a full year of inactivity. Off I went to the local women's gym and worked it off, little by little. (Janet's note: For more insights into the Seven of Pentacles, see the commentary for Mary K. Greer's BIT Snapshot "Discovering the Tarot" and my own "The Cracked Spring.")

**Nine of Swords,** redux: Once all the physical emergencies had been dealt with, fractures in my marriage showed up, followed by many sleepless nights, anxiety, pain, and frustration. The related psychological and emotional issues most likely triggered a number of new migraines. Ultimately, these fractures led my husband and me to confront issues that, in the end, led to a divorce. But there were many years of sleepless nights even *before* it became possible to imagine that divorce might be the outcome.

**Eight of Swords** and **Temperance:** I won't cover all that happened next, but now I feel that there are two major cards in play. The Eight of Swords represents the relatively minor restrictions this serious illness still can create in my life. I try not to be bound or restricted by it, but inevitably, it does happen. Acceptance is important here—someday I may be able to shed these swords, but for now, they're part of me.

The other major lesson is balance, depicted on the Temperance card. Our bodies are such an amazing creation, chemically and neurologically complex. Management of this illness requires artistry and maintaining my environment and physiology in a complex dance of stimulus and response. There is also emotional creativity required to blend it into my everyday life without becoming resentful, frightened, or burdened—even to see the benefits it may bring. I must learn to ask for help when needed, without dwelling too much on it day to day. I've learned to live self-sufficiently while allowing for some degree of interdependency.

## COMMENTARY

Except for the Six of Swords, a card Teresa associated with two decks (the *Robin Wood Tarot* and the *Thoth Tarot*), Teresa didn't have a particular deck in mind when creating her BIT Snapshot. A longtime member, and now owner, of the Yahoo Group "Comparative Tarot," she and group participants practice a method popularized by Valerie Sim, which evaluates one card at a time, comparing versions from a multitude of decks. In fact, the book *Tarot Outside the Box*, authored by Sim, is dedicated to this comparative process. Because she thinks "outside the box" by comparing the images from dozens of decks, Teresa has "created a sort of conceptual archetype for each card that doesn't necessarily use specific versions of them," as she told me. As you can see from her example, while the BIT Method can be used with any specific deck, this technique is equally useful for those who conceive Tarot cards in terms of a unifying archetype.

The usual image of the Judgement card, as Mark McElroy says in his BIT Snapshot, is a "classic image of the Day of Judgement." Although many Christians interpret this as a literal resurrection, this card can symbolically represent a "rebirth" via a transformative experience. In fact, the new life may bear little resemblance to the old one, especially if the old one was accompanied by extraordinary challenges such as chronic pain. Teresa likens the onset of her migraine to a "trial by fire," and though her Tarot reading portended success in her new venture, she felt the cards indicated this success would coincide with pain akin to giving birth. In her book *Jung and Tarot: An Archetypal Journey*, Sallie Nichols writes of the figure in the Judgement card:

> Although our hero appears to be redeemed, his life henceforward is not to be envisioned as one of perfect peace and everlasting harmony. He, too, must pay a price. His increased awareness will inevitably entail increased responsibility. His long trial in the dark dungeon is over; but he must now face the challenge of new light . . . Although he is now able to move about in the world as he chooses, he will find that his choices and values have changed during his confinement. His increased awareness may bring with it wider areas of choice and a more acute sense of responsibility.

Great pain can often birth extraordinary blessings and opportunities; however, we're rarely the same person after such experiences as we emerge on the other side of them with different values, expectations, and priorities.

In Rider-Waite decks, the Four of Swords shows an armored, prone figure with arms folded like a steeple, hands clasped together as in prayer. Some Tarotists see this imagery as a mausoleum and the figure as a deceased knight. In numerology, the number four often indicates stability and, coupled with the mental suit of the swords, can connote ceasing from worry or over-thinking. Others, like Teresa, often view this card as inactivity, recuperation after illness, isolation, or simply taking a break for a much-needed rest.

With the moon's eerie half-light, benign objects like trees, rocks, and foliage can take on a sinister appearance. Because of this ability to change how we see things, the Moon card can indicate confusion and fears that are often a part of challenging circumstances, like Teresa's.

Teresa mentions the Moon card again in the Six of Swords association, in connection with hormones. The earth's moon has long been associated with feminine cycles, which are also regulated by hormones, so the connection seems natural.

In many Rider-Waite–inspired decks, the Six of Swords depicts a huddled woman and child being ferried in a boat by a man. Because one side of the water is usually choppy and the other calm, many Tarotists interpret this card as escaping from a troubling situation or journeying on to improved circumstances. Like Mark McElroy, Teresa touches upon the *Thoth Tarot* equivalent of this card, titled Science, which can indicate the disciplines of medicine (both allopathic and alternative), as well as pharmaceuticals and an organized health regimen.

Teresa draws upon numerology to explain her choice of the Nine of Swords. This esoteric study of evaluating number qualities can yield additional insights into card associations, especially when the numbers are paired with a suit (swords, in this case). Her book *The Complete Tarot Reader* has great information on numerology.

In many Tarot decks, including the Rider-Waite, the Eight of Swords shows a blindfolded woman, who appears to be wrapped rather loosely with a white strip of cloth, surrounded by eight swords stuck into the ground. Like Teresa, many Tarotists see this images as connoting restriction of some sort.

In the Temperance card from the Rider-Waite, an angel pours liquid from one cup to another. The angel stands with one foot on land and the other in a body of water. In esoteric terms, this card is often associated with alchemy, while in modern terms it can be associated with chemistry. According to the companion book to the *DruidCraft Tarot*, authored by Druidry experts Philip and Stephanie Carr-Gomm, the word "temperance" is derived from the Latin *temperare*, which means, "to blend and harmonize opposing factors." In fact, the Carr-Gomms rename Temperance "the Fferyllt," which was the name of a group of Druid alchemists who lived in the mountains of Snowdonia. Commenting about alchemical development in light of this card, the Carr-Gomms note that it is a process of "uniting and combining different elements of the self to achieve wholeness, illumination, and a release of our creative potential." It makes perfect sense that Teresa selected this card to represent the dance of physiologically managing her migraines, maintaining emotional balance in the face of pain, knowing when to ask for help, and looking for the hidden blessings on her journey toward wholeness. Just as the ancient Fferyllt mixed their various powders and potions to create healing elixirs, Teresa blends various approaches in the pursuit of her well-being.

## YOUR TURN

— Have you ever experienced a crisis that restricted you in some way or kept you homebound? How did it affect your relationships? Your attitude? Create a BIT Snapshot using cards that seem to explain how you felt.

— Can you think of a friend, family member, or acquaintance that made the best out of a difficult situation, perhaps even to the point of discovering a new skill, finding a new passion, or embarking on a new life path? Which cards would you select to represent the individual and the circumstances?

— Recall a famous person with a physical limitation who learned to live with the restriction, even transcending it. Choose cards to symbolize this quality.

## LAWYERS, POLICE, A JUDGE—OH MY!
### *Wilma Carroll*

A few months ago, I received a summons in the mail informing me that I had to go downtown for jury-duty service.

I did not want to do it.

They can keep you at the courthouse for one or two weeks. You can't work, so money gets tight. And you are not even allowed to bring a cell phone. I had gotten out of it before by speaking my mind. I told them I despise lawyers. I was determined to get out of jury duty yet again. In the morning, I sat in the waiting room, chatting with two foreigners, a man from Russia and a woman from Paraguay. They had become American citizens and spoke English very well, but both were worried about understanding legal terms in English. After lunch, I was called as a potential juror for a case. Supposedly, two men had sold drugs to a Drug Enforcement Agency (DEA) officer. I was *not* going to sit on this case, I thought. So I had to go before the judge and tell her why I was unfit to be a juror.

Deck used: *Rider-Waite Tarot*

**Ace of Swords:** This card shows a sharp sword coming out of a cloud; the hand holding the sword is strong and forceful. This picture reminds me of the threatening summons I received in the mail. Show up or go to jail or be fined $1,000.

**The Tower:** Lightning unexpectedly strikes a tall tower, and everything is upset. In the same way, a jury-duty summons can upset your schedule and throw your life out of joint. I had to reschedule an accountant's appointment and a doctor's appointment. I was set to start a temporary job, relieving someone on maternity leave, but I had to postpone that, too.

**The World:** The name of this card always makes me think of travel and faraway places, so I chose this card to represent the foreigners with whom I talked. I love talking to people from other lands. It is like having the foreign country come to *me*—a very inexpensive form of travel!

**Ace of Wands:** A firm, but pleasant-looking hand comes out of a cloud, holding a wand with green leaves. The leaves, to me, symbolize growth. Travel is broadening and so was the interesting communication I had with these foreigners. It was amazing to me how well they had mastered English. To me, the Ace of Wands is good, clear communication, oral or written.

**Four of Swords:** The figure in the card is lying there, not going anywhere. He is waiting, unable to move, and praying to be released from the immobility. I chose this card to represent the interminable waiting, sitting around the courthouse, and praying to be excused—soon.

**Justice:** This card's robed figure, holding a set of scales, clearly represents a judge. I was called up before a judge to explain why I could not serve on the case.

**Nine of Swords:** The woman on this card is anxious and worried. She holds her head in her hands. "Oh my, my, my," she sighs. This image makes me think of my anxiety and fear of talking to the judge. I was shaking in my shoes, terrified; I could hardly speak. I am an articulate person, but not before a judge and with the prosecutors, defense attorneys, and court reporter surrounding me.

**King of Swords:** The guy in this card looks very authoritative; he rules with iron force (the sword). It's his way or the highway. This card makes me think of the police (or the DEA). So I was standing before the judge and the other lawyers, and I proceeded to talk about the dishonesty of the police. This dishonesty is true, in my opinion. If someone has a criminal record, that person can join the police force if the criminal record is expunged. To me, this rule means that people with no morals or values can become police officers and be paid (with *our* taxes) to uphold the law.

**Nine of Wands:** The character in this card is looking around, perhaps suspicious of something or others. He wants to hold on (holding on to a wand) to what he believes is right, and maybe even prove the correctness of what he believes in. This card reflects my mistrust of the system. "The system doesn't work," I said to the judge. "The criminal is protected, and the victim is treated like a criminal."

**The Devil:** This card shows a stereotypical devil figure, with horns and cloven hooves—a figure traditionally representing evil, manipulation, perversion, and no morals. I chose this card to symbolize those who represent what I feel to be a corrupt system. The judge and all the lawyers were furious with me because I criticized the system that *many* in their field have corrupted. I feel they know the system doesn't work, yet they insist on believing in it, lying to themselves and others. Now propagating that lie, to me, is the work of the Devil.

**Nine of Cups:** The fellow in this card is happy and satisfied with himself. It is a great representation of me when I was excused from the case and told I would not be called up for jury duty for another four years. Pleased with myself because I had spoken my mind by standing up to a judge and lawyers,

I treated myself to my favorite pasta dinner at my favorite Italian restaurant that evening.

## COMMENTARY

Notice how Wilma chose the Ace of Swords, King of Swords, and Justice in regard to legal proceedings. These three cards are often associated with matters of legality, including lawsuits, custody battles, subpoenas, judges, lawyers, contracts, mediation, judgements, and all manner of law enforcement.

When I consider the character of Fonzie from the TV show *Happy Days*, or the characters from S. E. Hinton's books *Rumblefish* and *The Outsiders*, I tend to think of the Knight of Swords; they are hell-on-wheels types that may likely find themselves on the other side of the law.

Interestingly, some Tarotists feel that the swords suit, as well as the Tower and the Devil, have a negative connotation and tend to interpret them accordingly. Many, however, feel that each card has the potential for positive *and* negative implications, depending on the question asked, the surrounding cards, and the feelings evoked from the card. For Wilma, her experience was mostly a negative one, so it's no surprise she chose four swords cards and two of what some feel are the most negative cards in the deck!

In addition, Wilma chose three nines for her BIT Snapshot. In numerology, the number nine is associated with a sense of achievement or conclusion. Again, depending on if someone chooses to factor in numerological considerations, nines could be a favorable finale or the culmination of aggravating circumstances. When I ponder Wilma's choices, I see her desire for a quick end to a difficult situation. Fortunately for her, this particular story ends with what some consider the "wish fulfillment" card of the Tarot: the Nine of Cups.

## Your Turn

- Have you ever received a summons in the mail to serve on a jury, or have you actually sat on a jury? If not, what about a required meeting with a school principal, mother superior, teacher, minister, magistrate, or other authority figures? Select cards to represent your thoughts and feelings about such figures, as well as any interactions with them.

- Do you know anyone who has gotten a parking, littering, or speeding ticket, or perhaps conflicted with the law? Re-create the circumstances using Tarot cards.

- Recall a famous criminal court case or notorious legal proceedings that made headlines or the history books, such as sensational custody battles, inheritances, divorces, libel lawsuits, copyright infringements, or breaches of contract. Which Tarot cards would you choose to represent the people and issues involved?

# Forget Going Out for a Cup of Coffee
### Riccardo Minetti

One day, on an Italian beach looking up at Mount Circe, I found myself doing a Tarot reading for a friend of mine. Out of idle curiosity, she wanted to know more about Tarot, and I had been teaching her the basics off and on for a few days. The reading happened by chance and more as an example of what Tarot could be all about than anything else. But it went deep—very deep.

We both skipped lunch that day, choosing to stay out in the sun for about an hour and a half, the cards of the *Etruscan Tarot* spread out on a beach towel. It was possibly the best reading I've ever done in my life. What was strange about it was that I felt that this person and I were meant to be friends, if I am any judge of these things. There was a mutual feeling of liking and being liked, of discovery and interest.

After the reading, all that changed. The ease we felt the day before was suddenly replaced by a respectful, and thoughtful, distance. That day, I came to understand that a revealing Tarot reading never leads to an invitation to go out for a casual cup of coffee. I was allowed to peer more deeply into her life than any acquaintance should. I learned a lot that day. There is always some cost for an intimate Tarot reading, but in the end, I think it was a fair spring price.

Deck used: *Etruscan Tarot*

**The Lovers:** *The lightness before.* This card speaks of a beginning friendship, an exchange of opinions and jokes—a general summery, sunny way to enjoy the day.

**Death:** *The reading.* It speaks of a pivotal, unplanned moment. The sunny day suddenly turned autumn serious.

**Nine of Wands:** *The distance.* This card speaks of what I felt later, without really understanding why at first. It was not just a sense of detachment. It was more a feeling that everything that needed to be said between us had already been said, that there was nothing more to add. It felt like a chilly winter evening.

**Justice:** *Regret and learning.* What if I hadn't done the reading in the first place, or if I had steered it away from the direction it eventually took? Since I think it was the best reading of my life, I suppose it was an important occurrence—and not just for me.

## COMMENTARY

I consider Riccardo's BIT Snapshot quite an enigma! Although I don't fully understand his associations, especially since the *Etruscan Tarot* features unfamiliar depictions of pre-Roman civilization in Italy, I find the mysterious quality of the result of his beachside reading irresistible, which is why I chose to include it in this book.

The Lovers from *Etruscan Tarot* shows a nude man and woman entwined in a blanket, and flowers grace the bottom of the card. The Death card depicts a kneeling soldier in black garb, clutching four arrows with one hand and dropping (or reaching for) some small, red unknown object on a short table with the other hand. A soldier bearing a shield walks leftward in front of a lattice of budding wands in the Nine of Wands. On the Justice card, a winged creature holds two animals by the throat: a leopard in the right hand and a stag in the other.

Personally, I can't fathom how Riccardo arrived at his personal meanings based on card imagery alone, but that's the beauty of the BIT Method. What each person "sees" for a particular card is right for them and may very well one day serve as an important connection or interpretation for future readings and contemplation.

I found Riccardo's use of seasons in his BIT Snapshot fascinating, so I asked him if the *Etruscan Tarot* correlated with the four seasons in some way or if he was just a fantastically poetic writer. He chuckled and replied, "It's just me. I often read that way. I find that the use of seasons or times of the day (morning, noon, evening) does help to convey the idea of increasing or decreasing energies in reading."

Complex decks like Joseph Ernest Martin's *Quest Tarot* factor in timing by using symbols to represent months and seasons. Martin correlates the Ace of Cups with spring by including tulips in the card, the Ace of Wands with summer by depicting a sunset, the Ace of Swords with autumn by showing fallen leaves, and the Ace of Stones with winter by including snowflakes.

Other decks and traditions assign the four seasons to the suits of the Minor Arcana (or aces only) but without a definitive correspondence. For example, the *DruidCraft Tarot* associates the Ace of Pentacles with winter, like the *Quest Tarot*'s version of the earth suit. Unlike Martin, however, *Tarot Tips* authors Ruth Ann and Wald Amberstone correlate the Ace of Swords with spring and the Ace of Cups with autumn. In his book *Tarot Plain and Simple*, author Anthony Louis also associates pentacles with winter, but correlates wands with spring, cups with summer, and swords with autumn.

Some Tarotists do readings involving timing and associate the Minor Arcana suits or numbers with times of the day, seasons, or length of time (such as days, weeks, or months). For example, one method for timing suggested in Teresa Michelsen's *Complete Tarot Reader* is to interpret a preponderance of swords as indicating days, wands as weeks, cups as months, and pentacles as years. The actual number on the card could indicate the length of each time period; for example, the Three of Cups could mean three months.

## Your Turn

— Recall a conversation or interaction in which it seemed like the flow was heading in one direction but then changed abruptly because of an offhand remark, unintentional button-pushing, or a penetrating line of questioning. Which cards would you choose to represent the energies/feelings before, during, and after the pivotal moment?

— Think of a time when you witnessed an unusual interaction between a couple or in a group of people. Perhaps the volume of their conversation, wild gesticulations, or mannerisms were over the top or just plain bizarre.

Perhaps you eventually discovered the reason for their behavior or just chalked it up to drugs, drunkenness, PMS, or mental derangement. If you were to invent a story about what happened, which cards would you select to symbolize the root of the unusual behavior, as well as the people, interactions, conversation, and eventual outcome?

— Can you think of a movie or book in which the entire story takes place within one season? Which cards remind you of that particular season and of what happened among the characters, around the setting, and in the plotline?

# THE STRUCK TOWER
### Joan Bunning

In the spring of 2001, I contracted to write an online Tarot course for beginners. The plan was for me to write the material in May and June and then lead the first session of the course in July. Students would do the lessons and exercises online at their own pace. They could also join an ongoing discussion group if they wished. My role would be to check in from time to time to answer questions and share my thoughts.

I was quite excited about the project and managed to finish my material in time for the course start date. When I was told the enrollment was in the thousands, my heart skipped a beat, but I felt ready to go and eager to see what would happen.

I quickly realized I could set my concerns aside. The discussion group proved to be a lively and helpful assembly of Tarot lovers from all over the world. There were complete novices, seasoned readers, and every level in between. Our one common feature was a curiosity about the Tarot and its potential as a tool for insight and growth.

By September, a real community had formed. That was the situation when the events of 9/11 occurred in New York City.

Deck used: *Rider-Waite Tarot*

**The Tower:** How completely this card captures the key moments of 9/11! It shows a powerful force striking a tower, causing those inside to fall. As I watched the events on TV, I felt awe and sadness at this vivid manifestation of the Tower archetype. The meanings of this card—surprise, sudden change, upheaval—were playing out before my eyes.

**Five of Cups:** I felt an immediate sense of loss that day—loss of innocence, loss of trust, loss of lives. I felt as I imagine the figure on the Five of Cups feels—wrapped in a black garment of sorrow, seeing something precious washing away.

**King of Cups/King of Swords:** In the context of the course, as the discussion leader, I knew I needed to step forward to help the group come together around this event. I decided to write an initial message of support and then trust that the community would gather round. I tried to draw on the active strengths of these two kings—cups for wisdom and caring, swords for communication. Kings take action toward positive goals that reflect their suits. These cards were role models for me at that time.

**Three of Cups:** Before 9/11, our group had formed a bonded online community. On that day and after, we drew on this community spirit to share our concerns and feelings about what was happening. The course gave us a welcome forum in this time of need, even if only in a small way. Indeed, talking about the Tower card helped us all to deal with the shock of events and gain some bit of understanding about them. We linked arms in mutual support as much as we could.

**Six of Swords:** As I went through the Tarot deck for this BIT Snapshot, I was surprised that I passed over so many cards that might seem to apply to

9/11: the Three of Swords, Nine of Swords, Ten of Swords, the Devil, even Death. Perhaps the passing of years has muted the sadness, but for me, now, the Six of Swords is the card that marks the aftermath of that day. Always, we must pick up the pieces, move on, and begin to feel hope again.

**The World:** September 11 was a world-shaking day. It changed the direction and course of countless lives. When I saw the World card, I knew I would have to select it because of the import of that day for all of us. But I was also drawn by the card's image of the woman within a circle of green. Being part of the discussion group at that time helped me rest within a circle of support that drew from the world at large. Being connected in this way to caring people far outside my immediate circle was reassuring and even inspiring.

## COMMENTARY

In Rider-Waite decks, the Three of Cups shows three women dancing in a circle, arms upraised while holding goblets, as if toasting an accomplishment or celebrating together. As Joan points out, this pleasant scene often indicates community spirit, camaraderie, and sharing feelings with a group.

Joan was surprised that she didn't pick cards often associated with grief, worry, anxiety, cruelty, or death. This kind of discovery is but one of the unexpected benefits of doing the Back in Time Method: realizing that the cards we *don't* pick for a BIT Snapshot can be as illuminating as those we *do* choose. For Joan, choosing the Six of Swords, with its figures in a boat being steered through the waters, reminded her that even after great tragedy, it is possible to move beyond the choppy waters of upheaval and sadness into calmer waters flowing with healing, grace, peace, and newfound wisdom.

## YOUR TURN

— Has there ever been a time when you found camaraderie, support, or solace from a group? Choose the cards you feel best represent your state of mind, those involved, and the circumstances that brought you all together. After you're done, take note of the cards you *didn't* choose and what they may say about the situation or your unique perspective.

— Individuals deal with loss and grief in varying ways. Can you think of a time when you witnessed someone experiencing unexpected circumstances that resulted in shock, sadness, confusion, or even outrage? Which cards would you choose to represent the situation?

— Can you recall a worldwide event that brought people together in a big way? Which cards reflect the event, those involved, the media reporting, and your personal reaction to the event?

# THE ARTS FESTIVAL

## *Janet Boyer*

Almost every year, my family and I go to a juried arts festival held on the expansive grounds of Twin Lakes Park. With rolling green hills, twin lakes, woodlands, and meandering paths, this scenic park hosts artisans from all over the United States during four days surrounding the Fourth of July. From glassblowers to jewelry makers, painters to woodworkers, calligraphers to sculptors, the variety of artistry is a treat to behold. There are vendors offering ethnic foods, fresh-squeezed lemonade, roasted cinnamon nuts, and raspberry sundaes. Renaissance and Civil War re-enactors dot the landscape, as do a children's craft area, storytellers, a petting zoo, ice sculptures, chainsaw wood sculpting, stilt walkers, and magicians. Bluegrass fiddlers, ragtime jazz pianists, musical troupes, and Andean flute players perform.

Deck used: *Universal Waite Tarot*, except for the Child of Worlds card, which is from the *Voyager Tarot*

**Six of Cups:** I chose this card because, as I noted in the sample BIT Snapshot in the introduction, it has ties to nostalgia and fond memories. More than a decade ago, my husband introduced me to this festival, and it was where he and I began seriously discussing coming together as a couple. We shared a lot during that initial visit, as well as during subsequent visits to the festival, engendering many fond memories for me.

**Ace of Pentacles:** This particular park is picture perfect. We've also been there sans the festival, and the atmosphere is wonderfully tranquil. When I see the Ace of Pentacles, I'm often reminded of those times when a person feels peaceful, at one with the world, especially in terms of experiencing or communing with nature, since aces (and the number one) indicate a sense of unity for me and the pentacles suit relates to the earth element.

**The Fool:** One of the first entertainers we encountered at the festival this year was a colorful jester on stilts. With his long hair and flowing beard, this merry young fool represented a local Renaissance festival, enthralling kids and adults alike, much like the harlequin jesters of old that entertained royalty with their antics and so often find expression in many Fool cards.

**Eight of Pentacles:** In many Tarot decks, the Eight of Pentacles shows an apprentice or artisan diligently at work on the eighth pentacle, while seven hang on a wall or lie somewhere in the vicinity. At the arts festival, we were surrounded by diverse artistry, including singers, musicians, illustrators, clothiers, actors, poets, soap makers, silversmiths, and landscapers.

**Three of Pentacles:** My son, Noah, visited the children's craft area and made a huge tissue flower out of the colors of his choice. With help from an attendant and my husband (I was busy taking the pictures), he created a lovely blossom that he later used as a shade from the sun. In the *Universal*

*Waite Tarot*, the Three of Pentacles shows an artisan working on a building while a man and a woman look on. This image reminded me of Noah's handiwork being supervised and aided by the help of my husband and the female attendant.

**Child of Worlds:** The whimsical illustrations of Pennsylvania artist James Browne caught my eye, and I ended up buying two of his prints, which he signed for me. His paintings included gnomes, fairies, Humpty-Dumpty, anthropomorphic trees and animals, and other fanciful characters. I couldn't help but think of the Child of Worlds card, subtitled the Player, from the *Voyager Tarot*, which is laden with images of childhood exuberance, creativity, and games. The Player is equivalent to the Page of Pentacles, and James Wanless writes in the companion book to the *Voyager Tarot*, "You are still in the child's world of Frisbees, baseballs, bubbles, and balloons where life is play." The Player's realm is the realm of the magical child, and the artist I met at the festival was obviously quite comfortable in such a world, judging by his expressive art.

**The Sun:** Although the day was indeed sunny, I chose this card to represent my son's reaction to the heat. Being fair-skinned, blue-eyed, and blonde like his mom (and like the child in the Universal Waite card), he's often sensitive to brightness and heat, especially when it's coupled with high humidity and even while he's wearing sunglasses, sunblock, and a hat. Although he enjoyed himself, he began to feel nauseated as the day wore on—and eating some greasy french fries later in the day sure didn't help. I often think of my son when I ponder the Sun, not only for the son/sun wordplay, but also because of his sunny disposition.

## COMMENTARY

I picked four cards from the pentacles suit for this particular BIT Snapshot. The pentacles suit, associated with the element of earth, often deals with the material realm, including the environment, nature, possessions, money, health, workmanship, and physicality. Considering that the festival was held outdoors with dozens of artisans in attendance, it's fitting that I was drawn to the pentacles suit to recreate this moment in time.

There have been incidents in my Tarot-reading experience when the Sun indicated literal sunburn or heat-related issues. In fact, depending on the surrounding cards, especially those from the suit of wands (particularly the Ten of Wands), I've seen this card depict burnout. I've also interpreted the Sun card, however, as robust health, joyfulness, a sunny disposition, playfulness, spontaneity, optimism, and general well-being.

## YOUR TURN

— Have you ever had a day when all was well in your surroundings? Or perhaps you visited a gallery, sprawling mall, festival, or convention where there was a dizzying display of artistry or products. Which cards would you select to represent your mood, the items you saw, the thoughts you had, and the people around you?

— Have you ever witnessed an uninhibited person or exuberant youth who seized the day with gusto? What were they saying, wearing, or doing? Select the cards to symbolize what was going on at the time.

— Is there a famous entertainer you can think of who captures the imagination of thousands, enthralling audiences with their particular talent? Choose corresponding cards to depict their art, mannerisms, audience reaction, or criticism.

# FLYING THE NEST
### Josephine Ellershaw

It happens all the time, but it was a first-time experience for *me*. Our children grow up and, at some point, leave home to make their own way in the world. Our family unit consisted of my mother, my son, my daughter, four dogs, three cats, and me. My father had passed on less than two years before. Our large home was melodically noisy and somewhat chaotic, filled with music, nomadic teenage friends, and an army of eccentric pets (who had become the ruling majority quite accidentally rather than by design). One fine day, quite unexpectedly, our world changed when my son flew the nest.

Deck used: *Gilded Tarot*

**Eight of Pentacles:** My son, Robert, is now a diligent scholar. This may sound like a rather ordinary statement, but, in actuality, it wasn't always this way. During his higher education, he completely changed route, from academic study to following his growing passion of playing bass guitar. This switch led to a contemporary-music course and new college—a change that initially caused me, as a parent, concern. ("You want to do *what?*") Yet gone was the apathy he had previously displayed toward school, replaced by enthusiastic motivation and self-discipline, as he completely dedicated himself to mastering his craft. Just like the apprentice in this card had seven pentacles displayed around him, Rob soon had results and achievements to show for his diligent work. And like the apprentice is shown working upon the final eighth pentacle, wherein lies the promise of his future, Rob is continuing to pursue his goals.

**Six of Wands:** Upon completion of the two-year course, Rob finished with distinctions, earning himself an award from his college. Then he received an invitation from his favorite tutors to join them in a new teaching project and an offer for a full-time place at his chosen university to continue his music studies. For me, this card typified his accomplishment: his efforts were recognized and applauded by others and seen as well deserved. As he crossed the stage at graduation, the words all parents hate to hear, words from many a long-past school parents' evening, rang in my ears: "could do better." I smiled with pride at his complete turnaround.

**Ten of Wands:** Because of his local commitments—teaching part-time, performing regular gigs, and pursing the full-time degree course—Rob had decided not to live on campus, but live with us at home. In theory, it sounded fine, but in practicality, the sheer logistics started to become a burden. The daily journey back and forth to campus was long and arduous for him, resulting in very early mornings and late nights due to his other commitments. We watched with some concern as he battled on.

NOTE FROM JANET: The man in the *Gilded Tarot's* Ten of Wands, as in many Rider-Waite–inspired Tarot decks, is burdened by an awkwardly held armload of sticks. Just as the man on the card is carrying as much as he can handle, Rob also had his hands full with all of his commitments.

**The Fool:** Rob's new plan probably shouldn't have come as an unexpected surprise, given our initial, and unheeded, advice concerning his plans. But when he joyfully announced he was moving to the town where the train station was situated (the train station was usually the third stage of his daily journey), we met the news with stunned silence. My mother's eyes met mine across the dinner table as he continued talking with great excitement about this new adventure, but we also recognized the naivete of his youth. (Adventurousness and the inexperience of youth are both commonly associated with the Fool card.) There was, of course, sense to his thoughts, but his timing wasn't good. More important, was he adequately prepared for the move? My daughter, Emily, broke the silence as she recognized her own possible and unexpected opportunity of getting his (larger) bedroom.

**Knight of Swords:** The energy of the events that followed was swift and chaotic, requiring clarity of thought amid some confusion. With the academic year well under way, it was now "all systems go" to put everything in place quickly, such as a house, furniture, and finances.

**Death:** Since this plan was a sudden one, I wasn't prepared mentally or emotionally for this transition. There was so much to organize!

The van arrived, we loaded the last of Rob's personal possessions, he hugged everyone, and suddenly he was gone. The house fell into an unusual silence as Emily, my mother, and I each disappeared to our own quiet corners of the house. The evening passed by with an unspoken sadness, and even the army of pets, who normally follow our every move, lay huddled in a heap in the hall—except for Robert's dog, who lay by his bedroom door, waiting. I fought against the burning sensation in my throat, as I realized that from this point, life would never be the same again. This change was inevitable, but I still wasn't prepared when it came.

**The Moon:** This card felt correct here on many levels. From the surface, there was much more depth to the situation than could initially be seen. We appeared to go about our normal daily life, yet each of us was experiencing so much more than we were saying. Emotions fluctuated back and forth, as we made the adjustment in our routine. Here's an excerpt from my journal reflecting these feelings: "Emily plays piano in the hall, but the competing bass line from upstairs is missing. She stops abruptly mid-piece, muttering how she never thought she'd miss him this much as she seeks the seclusion of her new room. I feel inadequate to answer and am reminded of the similar atmosphere in the house after my father died, but equally I curse myself for making such a comparison."

On reflection, I see there was a type of grieving process, but due to the circumstances, we dismissed it as illusionary. Ah, the deceptive light of the moon!

**The Empress:** With three women in the house, two of us mothers, it would be hard *not* to include this card, especially since the Empress is often considered the paragon of motherhood! We nurtured each other's spirit, and for me, this change provided valuable time alone with my daughter. I am reminded that part of a mother's function is letting her children go when the time comes so they can make the healthy transition into adulthood. All too soon, this transition would come for Emily as well. Meanwhile, we all played the role of "mother," as we took the occasional phone call from Rob seeking advice on washing-machine cycles, oven settings, or automatic bank payments.

**Ten of Cups:** This card shows a cozy cottage, two women sewing happily, and an orange tabby cat leaping to catch some thread; it reminds me of a "gathering of the clan." Obviously, Rob returned home to visit, although initially, due to his schedule, it took some months before he did. The house was again filled with music, laughter and love, bouncing pets, and the enjoyment of food and each other's company around the dinner table. We felt emotionally and materially fulfilled. All was well in our world!

**Wheel of Fortune:** And then, just as you think everything is nicely settled, so the hand of destiny turns the wheel of fortune. Teenagers! But that was the beginning of a whole new chapter, and another story.

## COMMENTARY

One thing I noticed about Josie's BIT Snapshot is that she chose three significant tens: the Ten of Wands, the Ten of Cups, and Trump 10, the Wheel of Fortune. In Tarot numerology, tens often indicate some kind of fullness or even excess. Josie was concerned about her son's burdens, while also feeling the paradoxical fullness of an empty nest. Something was filling that void, including feelings of wistfulness and uncertainty. But fortunately, the Wheel of Fortune came rolling back around again in the form of a happy, though temporary, reunion.

In numerology, ten as number isn't considered; rather, it is reduced to one $(10 = 1+0)$. And since ones are also beginnings, a ten card could indicate starting anew—the "higher octave" of an ace, so to speak. As with an ace, something is beginning, but with the addition of experience and (hopefully) wisdom. Thus, although aces can be seen as a blank slate or something highly original, tens can be seen as a new twist on a familiar idea or going back to the proverbial drawing board. For Josie, she is obviously still a mother and has opportunities to do some mothering, but it is a different form of mothering from when Rob was at home and still under her protective wing.

The Six of Wands in the *Gilded Tarot* shows a man riding a horse among a crowd, banners and flags waving. Like many Rider-Waite–inspired versions of this card, the image often reminds Tarotists of triumph and public acclaim (especially if the image depicts a cheering crowd), including commencements and inaugurations like Rob's graduation ceremony.

Because knights, especially ones coupled with the masculine suits of wands and swords, often connote swiftness, it makes sense that Josie chose the Knight of Swords as a "full speed ahead" card. By design, swords are sharp, and since the suit of swords is often associated with the mental realm, the Knight of Swords could certainly be seen as a sharp mind or cutting through murky circumstances with clear thinking.

The Death card rarely foretells actual death, but often represents times of transformation from one stage to another, much like a butterfly emerging from a chrysalis. Transitions such as divorce or a physical move can engender the pain of separation, just like that of a physical death. Rob's departure was a time of great transition for everyone in the family, even the pets. Although the only constant in life is change, we're rarely prepared for it and often experience a sense of loss, confusion, and emptiness in its wake. The Death card can also, however, connote a radical new "birth" into a stage of life or consciousness, and this can occur quite unexpectedly or through the squeeze of metaphorical birth pangs when we persevere through challenges.

## Your Turn

— Has there been a time when you've been gobsmacked by a change, even one that, by all accounts, could be anticipated as part of the natural order of life? Which cards would you choose to represent the situation?

— Do you know a parent who has experienced empty-nest syndrome? How did they cope? Have you ever witnessed someone dealing with an abrupt change, such as a job layoff, a "dream job" offer, or perhaps the departure of a familiar face? Choose cards to represent the people and reactions involved.

— Can you think of an incident in which the sudden departure of a public figure surprised, dismayed, angered, saddened, or thrilled the public? What happened, and which cards would you pick to symbolize the event?

## Selling House
### Phyllis Vega

About nine years ago, I put my house up for sale because I wanted to move to another neighborhood. A middle-aged couple made an offer on the house, and we agreed on terms, including the price. The day they were supposed to sign the papers, however, they backed out of the deal. About six weeks later, I had a call from a man who identified himself as a real estate agent. He said that he had someone who was ready to buy the house and asked me to have my agent prepare the paperwork. I was suspicious, because his buyers didn't ask to see the house. Finally, he explained that although he really was a real estate agent, he was also the son of the same couple who had almost bought the house and then changed their minds. His parents had decided that they did want the house after all. I called my real estate agent, and the sale went though without another hitch.

Deck used: *Albano-Waite Tarot*

**Four of Wands:** I chose this card to represent the house that I offered for sale in anticipation of a move to another part of town. In my book *Romancing the Tarot*, I include the following in my definition of the meaning of the Four of Wands: "the construction, sale, or purchase of a home." In the definition of the card in *Power Tarot* (which I coauthored with Trish Mac-Gregor), we said, "It can also mean a move—actual or metaphorical." The real association for me when I look at the card is the *chuppah*, which is the wedding canopy traditionally used in Jewish weddings. It consists of a cloth, sheet, or prayer shawl stretched or supported over four poles. It symbolizes the home in which the bride and groom will live. When I look at the card in the Rider-Waite deck, I see that image.

**Queen of Wands:** This is my card—my significator. In it, I see myself, with my little black cat, Pandora, waiting for news about the sale of the house. I envision the Queen of Wands as an independent woman. I switched to this card from the Queen of Pentacles after my husband died, at which time I adopted my black cat. The queen doesn't look like me, but the pictured cat looks very much like Pandora.

**Queen of Pentacles:** My real estate agent, Abby. I chose this queen for Abby because she is a very successful real estate agent, and I associate pentacles with money and property.

**King** and **Queen of Swords:** The potential buyers. Both the husband and wife did a lot of talking, and the wife had quite a sharp tongue, which I tend to associate with the Queen of Swords.

**Eight of Cups:** The potential buyers changed their minds, turned their backs on the house, and walked away—just like the figure on the card walks away from the upright cups.

**Wheel of Fortune:** The card represents a turning point that brings sudden, unexpected changes. The wheel turns and prospects improve.

**Knight of Swords:** The buyer's real estate agent/son. I chose the Knight of Swords for him because his parents were the King and Queen of Swords.

**Six of Cups:** A blast from the past, as the couple revisits previous plans and reconsiders their options. Also, the involvement of the couple's son may be related to this card.

**Justice:** With the woman holding the scales in this card, I see Justice as a judgement in my favor. The contract is signed, and one cycle ends while another one is about to begin.

**Ten of Pentacles:** With my financial goal achieved, I am able to move forward and buy a house in the neighborhood where I want to live. I see the Ten of Pentacles—with its image of several generations, a house, and ten coins—as the ultimate in financial security and firm foundations for a contented family life.

## COMMENTARY

In Phyllis's BIT Snapshot, she attributes court cards to all the individuals. Seeing court cards as representations of particular people is a common practice among Tarot enthusiasts. Although some readers feel that pages correlate with young children, knights with adolescents, queens with mature women, and kings with mature men, other readers feel that court cards can just as easily represent personality traits rather than gender or age.

Because the suit of swords is often associated with communication—and often with sharp tongues—Phyllis understandably relates this suit to the buyers and their son. Noting that the pentacles suit, also known as coins, can represent the material world, including money and property, she ascribes this suit to her agent.

Also practiced among some Tarot readers is the use of a significator card. A significator is usually a court card that a reader assigns to either him/herself or the querent. These associations may be made according to the astrological sun sign of the person or according to another method. Some readers pick significators randomly before the reading, while others, like me, use no significator at all.

## YOUR TURN

— Have you ever been involved in the buying or selling of a house, property, or other large possession? What were the events leading up to the sale, and how did the transaction turn out? Which cards would you choose to represent the people involved? The possession? Your thoughts and attitudes?

— Think of a time when someone you knew wanted something very badly—perhaps wishing to snag a good job, get a new car, win someone's heart, or move to a better neighborhood. Did they get what they wanted? How did they react? Which cards represent how they felt in the end?

— Do you recall a historical event where a country or leader reneged on a treaty or agreement? Alternatively, can you think of a situation in the entertainment world where someone made a commitment but backed out at the last minute? Which cards would you select to represent the people involved, as well as the circumstances that transpired?

# TREACHERY AT THE OFFICE
## *Wilma Carroll*

Many years ago, I worked as an executive secretary in the sales department of a prestigious financial magazine. Salespeople tend to be aggressive, but in this office, they were crazy, out of control. They were all running around on survival instinct, like primitive cave dwellers. Backstabbing and malicious, everyone looked over everyone else's shoulder, trying to get something on them.

In addition, my boss, the big-shot associate publisher, was a screamer. Nasty, sarcastic, and a nitpicker, he thought you could not do anything right for him. "Use your head!" he would snap. He ruled by terrorizing people. I sat next to his administrative assistant, who took pride in being a gossip. She was also a drug addict who offered cocaine to everyone in the office. I was trying to maintain a standard of decency and class. Instead, I felt eaten alive by this job: demolished, yelled at, abused, humiliated, and, eventually, terminated.

Deck used: *Rider-Waite Tarot*

**Knight of Swords:** This card makes me think of the angry boss. He was always looking for an argument, rushing into a conversation ready to fight, just to take his anger out on some innocent employee who was trying to do a good job. The figure in this card doesn't appear to be thinking clearly about what he is doing. He is just charging forward with fury and rage, controlled by his hostile emotions—just like my former boss. He would blame everyone for *his* mistakes. It was always someone else's fault. No matter what you did, it was wrong, dumb, or stupid.

**Page of Swords:** The figure in this card has always interested me. He is leaning one way but looking the other, so he doesn't appear to know in which direction he is going. To me, he appears paranoid, suspicious, defensive, sarcastic, and petty, and this attitude makes me think of the boss's immaturity and inconsistency. He didn't make sense; he was unreasonable. One day I told him the administrative assistant didn't do her work and that, instead, she stood around and talked to her friends all day or talked on the phone. The boss said it was my fault, that *I* should make her do her work. I reminded him that *he* was the boss and it was *his* responsibility, not mine.

**Queen of Swords:** This card, too, has always intrigued me. You do not see this woman's face, only her profile. This posture reminds me of the two-faced administrative assistant. She would give you a smile to your face and then stab you in the back. She loved to gossip and spread nasty rumors about people.

**Seven of Cups:** Look at all the cup choices in this card: illusions, delusions, and fantasies. The shrouded figure in the middle cup near the top, with arms sticking out—who is that? It's someone who is confused, someone who doesn't know who he/she is or can't face the truth about him- or herself. I chose this card to represent the administrative assistant, as well as her drug addiction and her confused identity. People who are mixed up, indecisive, and don't know who they are can't come to grips with their weaknesses, so they drink and drug. Druggies do not deal with reality; they're always in denial. They run from reality and create illusions about themselves and the world. The administrative assistant was always creating some fantasy, trying to make herself seem important, as if she were someone big. She was always trying to make herself important by giving herself fancy titles or bragging about her knowledge of confidential information. She also thought she had a lot of class. (Once, I told her that gossips do not have any class; they are *tacky*. She was speechless.) The truth is she was a loser who eventually got fired from her job because she was incompetent and always out sick (because of the drugs).

And the viewer in the Seven of Cups, that person in the picture looking at the images—all that is seen is the back of that person, we do not see a face. And that figure is *dark*.

**Seven of Swords:** Look at this figure in this card sneaking away. He looks crafty, cunning, clever, and dangerous. This appearance is clearly representative of all the backstabbing and deception in that office. You didn't know whom to trust, and people were shameless about their ruthlessness.

**Five of Swords:** In the Rider-Waite image of the Five of Swords, a figure holds three swords while two are on the ground. He appears to be smirking, and two other figures are walking away—one looks to have his/her head bowed. From my perspective, this is another card that implies cutthroat tactics. It reeks of violence and brutality—an excellent portrayal of that savage environment.

**Eight of Pentacles:** The man on this card is fully absorbed in his work. He is concentrating hard, diligently laboring. I chose this card to represent me, as I tried to do my work and mind my own business in the office.

**Eight of Swords:** The woman in this card is blindfolded. She is uncertain where to step—and it looks as though no matter where she steps, she cannot avoid stepping into mud. This image is another snapshot of me, uncertain as to how to deal with the barbarian coworkers.

**Four of Pentacles:** The guy in this card is holding on tightly, and so was I at the time. I was trying to hold on to my sanity and my job (I was making good money despite the abuse). I did not want to bring myself down to the level of the others, and at the same time I was trying to hold on to my dignity.

**Wheel of Fortune:** Everything in life is cyclical. Nothing is constant. Change is inevitable. Just like the central wheel in this card, sometimes you're up, sometimes you're down. Eventually, I was terminated. The administrative assistant was promoted and then terminated. A few months after that, the screamer boss was terminated. What goes around comes around.

## COMMENTARY

Wilma chose six cards from the swords suit. Swords are often associated with arguments, harsh communication, cunning, deception, and ruthlessness—the very things Wilma experienced at her former job.

When I was chatting with Wilma about the Seven of Cups, she mentioned that she's also seen this card come up for gays who cannot deal with their sexuality (confused identity). In our conversation, she contrasted the Seven of Cups with the Four of Cups, noting that the figure in the Four of Cups appears lost in a meditative reverie/daydream, while the figure in the Seven of Cups is lost in delusional fantasies, and sometimes delusions of grandeur.

Those of us who read Tarot professionally, like Wilma, often develop mental shorthand for some cards because they seem to appear in particular circumstances. In Wilma's experience, the Seven of Cups often shows up indicating some type of confused identity or self-delusion, or someone with their head in the clouds. Based on this BIT Snapshot, Wilma's gut reaction to this card is quite negative. For me, I've often seen this card as "analysis paralysis" (a frozen feeling when faced with too many options or choices) or taking the time to evaluate the contents of each of the cups in terms of personal values. For example, I tend to see the castle in one of the cups as "building a house on a weak/sandy foundation" (to paraphrase Jesus in the New Testament) or even building castles in the air. The jewels in another of the seven cups can represent money and finances, the laurel wreath public acclaim or ambition, the head with the closed eyes prayer or contemplation, and so on. While Wilma sees the shrouded figure in a rather negative light, I tend to see its bright pink aura indicating someone who needs to allow their authentic "light under the bushel" (once again, to paraphrase Jesus) to shine forth in the world. As you can see, there is truly no right or wrong way to experience and read the Tarot.

## YOUR TURN

— Have you ever been in a situation rife with gossip and conflict? Did you ever work for the "boss from hell"? Choose cards to create a BIT Snapshot of your experience.

— Recall a time when you observed a "what goes around comes around" type of situation. What was involved in the sowing, and the reaping? Was it instant karma, or was the harvest a long time coming? Which cards would you select to represent the people involved, as well as the outcome?

— Have you ever watched a movie about office politics or volatile group dynamics? Or can you think of a historical event or a situation from the headlines that featured such elements? Re-create what happened using the Tarot cards of your choice.

# LEARNING TO RIDE A BIKE
### *Janet Boyer*

A week before my son's ninth birthday, we bought him a bike as one of his presents. Despite being the first day of autumn, it was a surprisingly hot and sunny day when we took my son to the park to teach him how to ride his new bike. My husband patiently instructed Noah, cheering him on at every try. I decided to walk the track surrounding the park to get in some exercise on this lovely day. We had a great time, despite the fact that I encountered a creepy guy on the walking trail.

Decks used: *Universal Waite Tarot*, plus two cards from the *Housewives Tarot*

**Knight of Wands:** In the *Housewives Tarot*, this card shows a youth riding a bike (complete with a pot on his head as a helmet and a toilet plunger substituting for a knight's lance). For obvious reasons, I thought of this card to represent my son's energetic practice sessions. (Later that day, Noah was playing on the swings. Interestingly, he exclaimed, "Sir Noah to the rescue!" as he sailed high in the air. Knight of Wands, indeed!)

**The Hermit:** I chose this Universal Waite card to represent my husband, a gentle, wise, and serene person. As my son's "coach" for the day, he guided Noah with patient instruction, encouragement, and praise.

**Eight of Wands:** I see this card, with its eight speeding wands sailing through the air, as signifying "full speed ahead." I sometimes ponder this card when I want to embark on an exercise regimen involving walking in the park or on my treadmill—especially since ramping up my metabolism is one of my goals when I exercise.

**Five of Wands:** A local youth club was holding a soccer game in one of the fields at the park. Whenever I think of team sports, the Five of Wands comes to mind, especially in terms of competitive cooperation and "proving your stuff." This is because the Universal Waite image shows five youths swinging long, budding sticks, which appear to make contact in one instance. One phrase that comes to mind when I see the Five of Wands is "It's all fun and games until someone loses an eye," because playful roughhousing (or even verbal sparring) can quickly turn into anger, accidents, or hurtful words.

**The Magician:** As I was walking the park trails through a forested area, I noticed a guy in front of me acting suspiciously. The first time he turned around to look at me, I wasn't concerned. But after I rounded a bend and realized he was walking up a hill *backward*, looking my way the whole time, I made an about-face and worked my way back to my husband and son. In the *Housewives Tarot*, the Magician is depicted as a smarmy salesman selling a washer. Is he on the up-and-up, or is he trying to sell damaged goods to an unsuspecting homemaker? The Magician from this particular deck reminded me of the creepy guy with unknown motives.

**The Empress** and **the Emperor:** As the day wound down and my family enjoyed the swings, I sat on a bench and jotted notes, making an impromptu BIT Snapshot. (See? The BIT Method can be done anywhere!) I chose these two cards to represent myself at that moment. On one hand, I was the loving mother embodied by the Empress, enjoying my two guys as well as nurturing my current "baby"—this book. This fostering energy was balanced by her counterpart, the Emperor, a role I took on as I organized my ideas, adding structure to my creative inspiration.

## COMMENTARY

Although I tend to see my son as the happy, innocent baby atop a white horse, as depicted on the Universal Waite Sun card, the bike-riding lesson reminded me of the Knight of Wands from the *Housewives Tarot*. By exposing yourself to various Tarot decks, you expand your cache of imagery, giving you more to draw upon as a Tarotist.

No matter which deck you choose, each card has a continuum of light and shadow qualities, as I mentioned in chapter 1. This means that cards that appear negative can have positive aspects and that happy cards can have a dark side. For example, the nurturing, productive, creative mother exemplified by the Empress can turn into a smothering control freak or, in the worse-case scenario, an abusive "Mommie Dearest" like David Pelzer's biological mother in his book *A Child Called "It."* Some Tarotists read shadow and light qualities of a card based on reversals or elemental dignities, but you don't have to concern yourself with those practices for the BIT Method if you're unfamiliar with them. Just evaluate the cards based on your personal associations.

The Magician, in its light aspects, can represent focused consciousness and eloquence, as well as manipulating abilities and tools toward a specific goal. In its shadow, however, the Magician can be a deceptive individual with ulterior motives.

Quite a few cards in this BIT Snapshot are "fiery" in nature—all of the wands, the Emperor (associated with the zodiac sign of Aries, which is ruled by Mars), and the Magician (which displays a wand alongside the other three symbols of the four elements). In her book *Everyday Tarot*, Gail Fairfield has this to say about the suit of wands:

> Wands represent the growth and awareness of the *self* and all its potential. The identity and the ego are involved in the process of truly naming the self. With Wands, you are concerned with discovering your true self, apart from others. You are exploring who you are, alone, individually. You are discovering and uncovering pride in yourself and your creativity. You are sensing your own personal direction. You are naming the roles you want to play and the hats you want to wear. You are asking, "Who am I and where am I going?" and "How can I creatively express who I am?"

## Your Turn

— Do you recall a time when you were learning something new? What were you learning, and who or what instructed you? Pick the cards you feel best represent your learning process.

— Has there been a time where you saw someone trying to teach another person or group a new skill or concept? Who was involved, and what happened? Which cards would you select to represent the environment, people, actions, and conversations involved?

— Creepy people are, well, *creepy*. Can you think of someone from history or current events who made headlines because of their creepy persona or behavior? Is there a character in book or a movie that made your hair stand on end? Which cards would you choose to represent this person and the events surrounding them?

# UNREQUITED LOVE
*Zach Wong*

It was the year 2000. I had just moved to Melbourne from Adelaide, done my time at university, and was beginning my journey of creating the *Revelations Tarot*. I had found a job working in a call center and lived in a shared house with three complete strangers. I was also open to meeting as many new people as possible to grow my then-small circle of friends.

Jay (not his real name) was a friend of a friend I met clubbing. He had a dorky smile, gentle demeanor, and the saddest puppy-dog, blue eyes. He was also disarmingly friendly and simple in his approach to life. He was a counterpoint to me in many ways, and I was smitten.

Our friendship was uneasy because he always knew I was attracted to him. Unfortunately, this story of love does not have a happy ending because of bad timing and the distance that sometimes burdens the heart. It was a very important life lesson, however, because I learned about myself, and I still hold the experience dear, just as if it were yesterday.

Deck used: *Revelations Tarot* (designed by Zach)

**Six of Swords:** When I first moved to Melbourne, I had let go of many things in my past life in Adelaide. Like the journey of the card's figure, pushing through difficult water, my journey to a life in another state and city meant I allowed myself to be freer in terms of the mind and in terms of preconceptions. When I met Jay, he was already in a relationship, and I would never have dreamed of breaking them apart. But I was in a new environment, and

I felt I had nothing to lose. I let go of all the old ideas that held me back and kept me being a martyr to my friends and to myself. I was, however, cautious of repeating my past mistakes.

**Six of Cups:** Even after Jay broke up with his then partner, we remained only friends. I tried not to push it too much, because of failed relationships of the past. While the Six of Cups can indicate fond memories, the shadow image of this card in the *Revelations Tarot* shows a merman mentally tormented by arguing baby seahorses—a symbol of disturbing memories. My self-esteem was low from a series of unrequited loves and rejections. With each "interest" I approached, I was more cautious than before. The bad feelings of the past plagued my mind continuously. Jay wasn't doing much better. He had just come out of another failed relationship and was playing it slow. Over the next few months, we danced cautiously on the line between friendship and intimacy.

**Knight of Wands:** Jay and I are both fire signs; I'm a Leo, and he's an Aries. In an ideal situation, we would fuel each other and burn brightly as a couple. Like the knight in the card, however, we were both riders on an uncontrollable fiery dragon and couldn't seem to get it together. When I pushed, he pulled away. When he came back, I was reluctant to be hurt again. Whenever I tried to plan an exciting date or to spend time together, he was unavailable or unwilling. In the end, it wore me down, and I decided to cut my losses. Months later, he decided to come back to me and proclaim his undying affection, but I had moved on in my mind and in my heart. He sent me flowers. He kept calling. He sent e-mails. He was determined. It was all frustratingly out of sync.

**The High Priestess:** Many Tarotists interpret the High Priestess as the keeper of mysteries or secrets, and there were a lot of hidden and unspoken issues between us in the months of our courting. Intuitively, I know that if we had taken the time to understand, perhaps it wouldn't have become the painful experience it was. When Jay decided to come back and pick up where I had left him, he confessed something very personal to me. I never realized that he grew up in an environment where the "Asian kid" was always belittled and put down. He came from a background where my ethnicity was different and unattractive. His reluctance during our time together was due to him trying to resolve his feelings toward his own upbringing and me. He didn't tell me this until it was much too late. Perhaps if I knew, I would have persevered. All I know now is that he needed the time away from me to deal with these issues.

**Five of Swords:** After I cut my losses, there was a period of constant doubt as the failure of the situation played repeatedly in my head. I would take each moment we spent together and then psychoanalyze it to shreds. I found myself playing the victim and the martyr at the same time, justifying why I did not need him in my life, and then asking why I was not worth his time and effort. As part of my own self-therapy, I would play reaffirming music repeatedly to help myself deal with daily life. My song choice became so repetitive that a colleague at work can no longer listen to the Britney Spears song *Stronger* without feeling ill. (Granted, my choice in music was questionable.)

**Page of Wands:** After Jay, I made many stunted attempts at relationships. I found myself trying to get into the dating scene, but halfheartedly. I found myself being reclusive from the scene in general. I allowed the feelings of self-doubt to creep into my work, my art (I even stopped working on the Tarot deck for a while), and my general outlook on life.

**Five of Pentacles:** This card indicates starvation for comfort in many forms, but eventually, I grew numb to the longing for physical contact. I had shut down the idea of intimacy.

**Three of Cups:** Coincidentally, I started drinking at this time. In the *Revelations Tarot*, this card in its negative association connotes loss of control and excessive drinking. Back in Adelaide, I was never one to drink when I went out with my friends. I was always the responsible one driving them home at the end of the night. Never one to do things in half measure, however, I recall the night I attempted to find out what my limit was. In the controlled confines of home, nine vodka mixers in two hours found me hunched over the toilet bowl. The sensation was new to me, as I had never drunk so much that I couldn't feel my cheeks. After that episode, I paced myself better when I went out. I became a social drinker to ease the pain and difficulty of social inhibitions when meeting strangers.

**Nine of Cups:** This is a "positive vibes" card reflecting the feeling of emotional connection with those around me. Eventually, after months of meeting new people and forgetting about Jay, I found contentment in myself because I had supportive friends. The time I spent apart from Jay made me understand that, regardless of my failures, life does move on without me. When he eventually came back to me, I was emotionally capable of rationalizing my feelings for him. We spent a night together (upon his insistence), and I lay there in the aftermath feeling empty. Too much time had passed between my initial momentum and his journey of self-realization. In the end, we acknowledged the bad timing and both moved on.

**Nine of Wands:** Although I hold the idea of Jay very dear to my heart, I have accepted that the possibility of us being together again in the future is next to none. Since we first met, we have grown into different people.

I often see him out and about, and I keep tabs on his current long-term relationship. It is a struggle for me, though, because he's found happiness with someone else (who, ironically, is another Asian guy), and I continue to be single and wonder "What if?" on my loneliest nights. As I write in the companion book to the *Revelations Tarot*, "[T]his card advises to fight on once again and to draw on whatever resources you have left. Difficulties may continue to dog your path, but your efforts will carry you through." I do live in hope every day that wisdom and fate will cross my path with someone special.

## COMMENTARY

In addition to its sensuous curvilinear strokes, striking art nouveau–style images, and vibrant, luminescent stained-glass surroundings, Zach's innovative deck is one of the only ones that includes reversals in the actual imagery. If you're new to Tarot and would like to try your hand at reversals, *Revelations Tarot* would be an excellent deck for experimentation. This deck's Six of Swords, for example, shows a figure in a boat with three swords; this image is reflected in the water, creating three more swords for a total of six.

According to Zach, the theme of destitution plays a major role in the Five of Pentacles card. He writes of this card, "The anguish and loss of energy and drive is accentuated through the twisted poses of the impoverished bodies on this card." The Three of Cups shows three laughing merpeople in a sea of lavender and blue, raising their cups as they spin continuously. Of the reversed image of this card, Zach says of one of the mermen: "He loses control and has drunk too much. He spins with them but cannot hold on for long . . . The background on the bottom of this card is littered with bottles, indicating overindulgence in celebration. The excessiveness can take its toll, as indicated by the merman who cannot even keep his eyes open."

The Nine of Cups in the *Revelations Tarot* depicts a smiling merman before nine golden cups. Zach writes of this figure: "He basks in the contentment of personal fulfillment. His radiance comes from inside him, and everything seems to dance around the song of his heart . . . He has reached a personal and emotional contentment with himself. The fish circle harmoniously around him, reflecting his happiness."

In the Nine of Wands card, a determined warrior summons an internal energy represented by a fierce-looking dragon. Although the battle temporarily disheartened the weary warrior, he draws upon fiery defiance from within to persevere.

In his original BIT Snapshot, Zach reversed the Six of Swords, Six of Cups, Knight of Wands, Page of Wands, and Three of Cups. Because I chose not to deal with reversals in the snapshots, I have left the reversal notations off the card choices. I asked Zach, however, for his thoughts on reversals and the light-shadow continuum of each card. He had this to say:

> In the world of black and white, light and shade, darkness and brightness, people often find themselves dividing matters into easier, more manageable (and sometimes simplistic) concepts. Life is not that easy or simple, though. Appreciating both sides of a spectrum allows one to understand any issue at hand before making a decision. Reversals are merely a varying degree of the theme highlighted by the card. Sometimes they may be the polar opposite; sometimes they may be just a subtle twist. The message of a reversal should be as applicable as the right-side-up image.

After Zach completed his BIT Snapshot, he told me that he found it curious that he started with two sixes and ended with two nines. When I asked him what he made of that, he noted:

> Sixes are often a pivotal point. Nines are often a point of contentment. In a linear sense (as with Jay's journey), it occurred during a time when I had moved from one stage of my life to another. The nines just highlight the conclusion/closure I brought

within myself about the situation after all that time had passed—a neat "Hollywood" ending.

The Five of Swords in the *Revelations Tarot* deck shows a figure about to commit hara-kiri, which is a Japanese ritual of committing suicide because of some type of failure or dishonor. In the deck's companion book, Zach notes about this card: "The loss of control over your own success and the amount of anguish you experience as a result will depend upon your spirits . . . Breakups in relationships may also be linked to not meeting the other's expectations or even your own."

Regarding the Page of Wands, Zach writes, "Unable to get in touch with your inner powers, creative energies seem to spurt out in sparks with nothing else to show for it . . . There may be creative or artistic difficulties, or an instability of emotion from stress and general unhappiness."

## YOUR TURN

— Recall a time when you were plunged into a new situation. Perhaps you made a physical move like Zach, or you began a new school, job, or relationship. Select cards to represent your thoughts and feelings about the experience.

— Have you ever witnessed a relationship that just didn't work out—or maybe a friendship or romantic connection that just seemed out of sync in some way? How has that situation affected your view of relationships in general, if at all? What cards would you choose to represent the people, actions, and choices involved, as well as the conclusion (or current state) of the relationship? If you don't know how it all ended, imagine a likely scenario and choose correlating cards.

— Bring to mind a historical situation, current event, movie, book, or TV show that involves distrust, confusion, or fear among disparate people.

Which cards would you choose to represent any cultural bias, ideological clashes, or physical confrontation?

# THE YEAR OF THE TOWER CARD
## *Lisa Hunt*

September 11, 2001, left an indelible impression on everyone, the tragic events affixing themselves in our collective psyches. For many people, 2001 was a year of changes on both a collective and personal level. Whether 9/11 precipitated personal change or was the impetus for change, people like me saw their own worlds turn upside down as the towers collapsed into a devastating heap.

For me, 2001 was a year of initiating heartache and divorce, but it also included graduate school, new projects, and meeting the love of my life. As painful as it is to reflect on some of the sadder moments, I look back on it as a year of tremendous growth. For this BIT Snapshot, I've chosen to use my *Animals Divine Tarot*, a project that I began working on around this time of great personal change. What ensued was one of the most positive, prolific periods of my professional career.

Deck used: *Animals Divine Tarot* (designed by Lisa)

**Three of Swords:** By 2001, my first husband and I had become estranged. We both felt at a crossroads, our daily lives together having lugubrious overtones. The things that had brought us together in the first place no longer served up magical interludes. We tried everything to make things work, but with each passing day, our lives become more stultified and uninspiring.

**The Tower:** My husband moved out one month before 9/11. We were just attempting to reconcile when the now-infamous events unfolded. Our consciousness was fully awakened, and we realized that we were building reconciliation on illusionary pretenses. There was no way to rebuild a solid foundation of conjugal happiness. We were irrevocably broken.

**Challenge:** The months that followed were filled with heartache and insecurity. I had spent many hours not just mourning the failure of my marriage, but also the end of all I had ever known. My repressed sadness and anger flooded through me; I thought I would never feel normal again. These feelings coincided with the feelings of helpless rage that gripped our country at the time. I was on emotional overload, but I knew I had to get through those dark days.

**Death:** After months of reeling from emotional blows and the lingering sadness surrounding world events, I started to feel better. I literally woke up one day and felt like a different woman. I began to come to terms with the death of my old life and was excited about the chance for a new beginning.

**Queen of Swords:** Great changes in my psyche were making themselves evident. I started to embrace my independence. With my newfound emancipation, I went and bought myself a new car. I was a warrior woman as I negotiated a good deal and drove out of the dealership feeling as though I could do anything. I also poured myself into my work, supplanting loneliness with occupation in the studio, a time when *Animals Divine Tarot* began to take form.

**Ace of Wands:** What ensued was a surge of creative and intellectual drive. I painted with an almost obsessive hand, allowing mellifluous brush strokes to serve as a catharsis. I felt strength in those paintings; a new maturity emerged, and my art took on a depth previously unexplored. It was wonderfully liberating and empowering!

**The High Priest:** During this period, I pursued graduate studies while simultaneously teaching classes at an art college. I immersed myself in academia and derived great satisfaction in higher learning. My life was healing, and everything around me began to blossom in vibrant color.

**Six of Wands:** The summer of 2002 fueled further transformation. I took control of my life, felt financially secure on my own accord, and started to come out of my self-imposed cocoon. I planned art- and book-related events. I felt victorious in my newfound independence and no longer yearned for the routine of my former life. Like the caterpillar on the Six of Wands, I had metamorphosed into a woman I'd always hoped I could become.

**Ace of Cups:** One night I did a book signing at a local New Age store. I dressed confidently and glowed as I exchanged words with the lovely people who attended the event. Lo and behold, I met a man whom I connected with instantly. I was not looking for him, nor do I think he was looking for me. But my heart reopened (ever so cautiously), and I intuitively felt he was someone special. And I was right—he later became my husband and someone with whom I truly feel I have been able to shine.

**Nine of Cups:** I chose the Nine of Cups because it is the perfect summation of my journey through "the year of the Tower card." Despite all of the obstacles and challenges that I encountered along the way, I learned that, by accepting change and evolving through times of crises, one can grow and become a better, stronger person. What had started out as a year of turmoil and devastation evolved into a great period of reawakening, newfound love, and ultimately a heightened sense of joy.

## COMMENTARY

In the *Animals Divine Tarot*, the Three of Swords card depicts a vulture sitting in a tree. In the deck's companion book, Lisa writes that the keywords for this card include "turmoil, sadness connected to past events, lack of communication, possible relationship troubles."

Lisa chose the Native American thunderbirds to embody the energy of the Tower card for her deck. Of this card, she writes:

> The arrival of thunderbirds is symbolic of change that may have both destructive and beneficial qualities. They awaken with their thunderous attributes and illuminating flashes. Their forces pierce through any residual self-illusionary towers that we may have built our ego upon. We are struck with the revelation that our lives must be reconstructed in order to fully integrate all the various aspects of our being. The raw elemental forces of the thunderbirds expose all the truths about ourselves, even aspects that we would rather relegate to the far reaches of the unconscious.

In the *Animals Divine Tarot*, Lisa renames the Devil card Challenge, replacing the familiar horned figure with the Welsh horse goddess Rhiannon. Many deck creators rename cards to reflect the theme of their deck, world-view, or spiritual path. The diversity of choices found among Tarot decks, such as that of the *Animals Divine Tarot*, adds even deeper layers to the BIT Method. When I asked Lisa to elaborate on her Challenge card, she wrote:

> First, I didn't want this deck to have overt religious conno-tations. The Devil card is based on Christianity. I don't have a problem with that, except I was looking for a more universal application that circumvented a particular religious connection. I love the Challenge card—it is such a bold, brave, courageous card to reflect on because we all have to confront our shadows eventually. And in the context of depth psychology, in order to individuate and attain a sense of "wholeness," we must deal with the devil/shadow! I see Challenge as a pathway to balance—confronting the dark in order to see the light. It's

the Darth Vader card of the Tarot, if you will, and I've always found it fascinating that it is planted in the middle of the Major Arcana—right after Temperance and before the Tower.

It is a reminder that dark forces are always with us, and we had better learn to assimilate the shadow, process it, and deal with it. Thus, we become stronger, because we're going to need all the strength we can get along our journey before being handed the Tower card (if you want to dissect the cards in consecutive order). If you notice, Rhiannon looks strong and proud on her horse. She has to go through a horrific ordeal of being accused of killing her child then sentenced to carry visitors on her back to the castle while telling them of her supposed infanticide before she is truly exonerated. But she comes out stronger, wiser, and, hopefully, better equipped to deal with her shadows. As I said, I love this card even though most people dread it. It's a card that forces one to grow—no more looking blindly the other way!

To represent Death in the *Animals Divine Tarot*, Lisa chose the Inuit goddess Sedna to symbolize the idea of transformation, renewal, and new beginnings. In the companion book, Lisa conveys the legend of Sedna and how she was transformed from mortal maiden into the supreme deity of the undersea world of Andluven.

For the Queen of Swords, Lisa aptly chose the beloved Greek goddess Athena, who sprouted from her father's (Zeus's) brow fully armored and is often associated with artisanship, wisdom, strength, and skill.

The brilliant firefly is Lisa's choice to represent the Ace of Wands, a creature she associates with abundant creative energy. She writes, "Fireflies illuminate the night sky as they gravitate to the crystal-topped wand. Fireflies provide inspiration and serve to initiate a period of new ideas. They pierce the dormancy of the night's darkness with their flashing abilities. They possess a magical quality and mesmerize viewers with their unique ability to generate light in a rhythmic pulse."

In the *Animals Divine Tarot*, Lisa renames Trump 5 (often called the Hierophant) the High Priest, correlating this card with the elephant-headed Hindu god Ganesha. The various symbols painted in this image symbolize higher culture, attainment of knowledge, and the never-ending quest for understanding.

Many Tarotists associate the Ace of Cups with the beginnings of love, and Lisa is no exception. Selecting the seal to embody the energy of this card, Lisa observes of the imagery: "Seals are animals that inhabit both watery realms and the shore, thus symbolizing the bridge between inner emotions and outer expression . . . Their inquisitive nature represents the openness to new ideas and beginnings. They are willing to plunge into the waters of new possibilities, allowing the heart to act as a compass on their travels."

I was intrigued by Lisa's choice of the Nine of Cups and asked her why she chose that card as opposed to the Star, a card many Tarotists might choose to represent peace and blessings received after chaos. She writes:

> I drew on pure instinct and felt that the summation of my emotional growth was just that—*very emotional* (thus the cups choice)! I arrived at a good emotional place, but I was keenly aware (given my experiences from a past relationship that failed) that happiness is not a given and not something to take lightly. Without the trials and tribulations along the way, we would not be able to appreciate those moments of basking in the light. I felt the Star would have been more indicative of a "dreams coming true" scenario on a grander scale, more detached from the day-to-day aspect of what I was feeling in my life at the time. I was content with feeling happy with my new love and new life, but I was also cognizant of

the fact that I still had a lot of work to do and that there was still a lot of emotional repair work to get through. I believe that residual sadness sits in the wells of our inner life for a long, long time. Even after marrying my second husband, a certain amount of sadness would surface from time to time because "the year of the Tower card" was such a dramatic and traumatic year for me. I'm glad it is still present in my psyche because it offers a reminder to appreciate the moment and embrace the good fortunes that I have been blessed with in subsequent years.

I wanted to emphasize emotional wellness, rather than focusing on the idea of acquiring a sense of wholeness. I wasn't *quite* there, at the wonderful Star card at the time. I was still taking things day by day. I guess I do connect more with the Star card now, but not then.

## YOUR TURN

— Recall a year that was "the best of times and the worst of times," to quote Charles Dickens. How did you navigate life's roller coaster? Select cards to represent the ups and downs, as well as what exited—and entered—your life as a result.

— If popular statistics are to be believed, half of all marriages end in divorce. Which cards would you pick to represent the concept of divorce? If you know someone who has been through a break-up, which cards reflect the circumstances involved?

— Most everyone knows Darth Vader from the *Star Wars* movies. If you had to pick a character or person to represent the Devil, who would it be and why? Which cards would you select to reflect their persona and actions?

# No Hell

*Janet Boyer*

From the time I was a small girl, I felt a connection to the Presence some call God. This connection was unusual, because my family didn't go to church at the time. Yet I felt closeness to God, often talking to "him." I begged my mom to take me to church, which she did, and I eventually acquired an olive-green leather King James Version Bible. I won the bible in a "sword drill," a Sunday school game where the teacher would call out a verse in the Bible and the students scrambled to be the first one to find it, then to stand up and read aloud the correct text.

As I devoured the Bible, I couldn't understand the concept of a supposedly loving God sending anyone to hell. I used to get angry when I read the verse asserting that hell was made for "the devil and his angels," but not humans; yet, humans could end up there regardless if they didn't ask Jesus to be their savior (or so the preacher said). As I sat fuming in my bedroom, I asked God, "How can this be? If you're so powerful, how can it be that you created a place called hell for one intention, but then—oops!—it became a place of torment for people?" Every time I asked this question, I "heard" a voice that said, "One day, Janet, you will know."

This internal argument with God, especially about hell, went on for years, even after I entered Bible college to study to become a minister. After college, I became ordained and co-pastored a Pentecostal church with my first husband. We were pastoring in a new area about an hour away from where we both grew up. We became friends with the pastors and congregation of a nearby church, sometimes guest teaching for services.

I became close friends with the other church's assistant pastor and many of the congregation members. After a few years, my friend and his wife went on to be the main pastors of the congregation. My friends were with me through thick and thin, including my first husband's diagnosis of leukemia, hospital-ization, rigorous treatments, relapse, and eventual death. We remained close even after I moved an hour away. After I remarried, my present husband and I traveled an hour one way to attend church to be with our spiritual "family." They rejoiced with us when I became pregnant and held a lovely baby shower in our honor.

One day, the son-in-law of one of the congregation members came to preach. He was a young itinerant minister with an unusual, but fascinating, teaching style. His teaching seemed to convey wisdom beyond his years, and I eagerly soaked it up. Attending church three times a week since I was a child, mandatory Monday through Friday chapel services at college, intense theology classes, rigorous personal study, and frequent teaching left me with an "already heard it/know it" attitude toward 99 percent of Bible teachers/ministers. That this minister captured my attention so completely was quite a feat at the time.

After church, many of us went over to the visiting minister's in-laws' house for dinner and conversation. There was lots of laughter and sharing. I ended up asking the minister one of my nosy questions—I can't even remember what it was, at this point—at which he looked at his mother-in-law and asked, "Should I tell them?" The minister went on to tell us that he didn't believe in a literal hell and quickly, but thoroughly, gave us the scriptural, linguistic, and historical reasons why he felt this way. I "heard" a voice in my spirit say, "Now, Janet, you finally have your answer."

I felt an indescribable sense of peace and clarity. It seemed so simple—and so obvious! I even declared, "Wow, I felt like I went to a spiritual chiropractor!"

My friends the co-pastors and the rest of the congregation present at the dinner (other than his in-laws), however, weren't so thrilled with this revelation. You see, they'd had no idea of his "heretical" theology before he guest-preached at the church. Because I had even *considered* that the minister's theology might be correct, my friends shunned me. Their behavior became so bizarre, and my husband and I became so uncomfortable, that we left the church a few weeks after that fateful day. Our friends cut off their relationship with us to the point that the co-pastor—one of my closest friends for years, so close that he was like a brother—forbade his twelve-year-old daughter from contacting me (she tried to call me on her own one day to wish me a happy Mother's Day).

Deck used: *Universal Waite Tarot* and *Lo Scarabeo Tarot*

**Ace of Swords:** I chose this card to represent my childhood anger toward God about the unfairness of hell and the suffering of humanity. The single, upward-pointing sword reminds me of "giving the finger," which I sometimes did in my room behind closed doors toward this ridiculously contradictory deity that I feared and loved.

**The Hierophant:** I often see this card as "the system," especially in terms of religion. I've come to associate this card with bearing the power of the "tribe," which often controls who is in—and out—of its special circle. Those that defy the decrees of the Hierophant (whether within the confines of a church, denomination, club, family, or culture) usually pay the price by becoming outcasts, or even scapegoats. The moralizing right and wrong stems from his pious decrees (written, spoken, or unspoken).

**The High Priestess:** The "gospel of inclusion" was heresy to my former friends and is a somewhat secret doctrine within Christianity. One reason this doctrine of universalism was largely unknown in Pentecostal circles at the time (despite the widespread historical tradition) was the consequences of believing and preaching a gospel that condemned *no one*. While I view the Hierophant as part of organized religion (which, unfortunately, tends to exclude those it considers to be undesirables), I think of the High Priestess as one who wishes to include all—whispering her secrets to those who quiet themselves to hear the still small voice that's ever present.

**Five of Pentacles:** My favorite Bible passages to teach as a minister were those dealing with self-righteous Pharisees. In Jesus' world, this group of religious leaders made it very difficult for average folks to reach God, and the Pharisees were the *only* people Jesus ever slammed in his ministry. Every time I see this card, I think of a song by the Christian band Petra titled "Rose-Colored Stained Glass Windows," which speaks about the "locked doors" of churches that keep out anyone deemed "unholy" or "tainted," while the leaders of these churches hoard the "light" for themselves as they refuse to behold and remedy the suffering of others.

**Four of Pentacles:** In the Universal Waite deck, this card shows a man clutching a coin to his chest, with a coin under each foot and one on his head. During one of the last services we attended in my former friend's church, he called up the church board (made up mostly of his relatives) and asked them to stand in front of him as a "spiritual barricade." The board president prayed a very odd and loud prayer about protection for the pastor (from the devil's wiles or some such). Their unusual theatrics reminded me of the man in this card who holds tightly to his belongings, seemingly fearful that someone will try to steal them from him or possibly destroy that which he worked so hard to obtain and maintain. In the *Lo Scarabeo Tarot* version of the Four of Pentacles, a man sits smack-dab in the middle of a walled fortress, clinging to a coin—much like the congregation members who tried to keep any insidious influences from tarnishing the "treasure" of (their version) of "the truth."

**The Tower:** The "bolt from the blue" represented by the lightning is an apt symbol of my spiritual chiropractic adjustment. My new perspective destroyed the theological tower built up by clergy, my theological studies, and years of reinforced belief. However, my newfound illumination cost me my reputation and friends as I was forced out of my beloved spiritual community and active ministry.

**The Hanged Man:** I chose this card to represent the complete turnaround of my perspective. While the fallout of my new ideology resulted in the Tower of rejection and upheaval, there was spiritual peace and clarity that defied logic. I felt as if I had been reborn, that the questions I had wrestled with for years were now answered. I no longer had to struggle and strive for answers, because they were coming in stillness and silence. Like the Hanged Man resting upside down with a peaceful look on his face, I was willing to wait in the place of not knowing until understanding came.

**Three of Swords:** Having my friend tell me that my mere consideration of a new theology made me a heretic grieved me. But when he continued to shun me and turned everyone in the congregation against me, it cut deeper than almost anything I had experienced in my life. The wounding from a faithful friend cuts deep, so the saying goes, and it took me many months to heal from this rejection. I felt as though my heart were ripping out, and the card image of three swords impaling a bright red heart over the backdrop of a gray, rainy sky captures my hurt and bewilderment.

**Death:** Although my former spiritual beliefs passed away, I entered a new path that led me to where I am today. There is no way I would have touched a Tarot deck in my old life, let alone consider that there are vibrant spiritual truths in other faiths and traditions. For me, it has been well worth enduring the pain and loneliness caused by the disapproval of the Hierophant, the locked church doors of the Five of Pentacles, and the grief of the Three of Swords so that I could have the life-affirming vocational and spiritual experiences that have brightened my way on this unexpected journey.

## COMMENTARY

When I was in college, one of my theology professors taught us about *gezerot*, a Hebrew word describing the hundreds of laws erected as a "fence" to keep people from getting anywhere close to breaking Torah laws in Judaism. When I think of the religious formality of the Hierophant in the Rider-Waite, I sometimes think of all the "laws" (spoken and unspoken) that ministers and denominations create to keep people in line or to prevent them from breaking accepted rules.

The Ace of Swords reminds me of focused power and cutting ability. While this card can relate to an idea, ideal, or act of communication, I'm reminded of how Christians refer to the Bible as a "sword." This doubled-edged sword has been used for centuries to persecute those who believe differently, sometimes to the point of excommunication or even death, as seen in the Inquisition, the Crusades, and the Salem Witch Trials. The concept of no hell was such a threat to my former friends that they chose to use their "sword of truth" as an excuse to reject my husband and me and brand us as heretics.

The Five of Pentacles reminded me of my former friends, who would actually help the suffering and the poor, as long as the poor believed as they did (or at least were good candidates for conversion). They acted like modern day Pharisees, willing to throw away a deep and abiding friendship on the basis of a mere theological concept. Jesus once called the Pharisees "white washed tombs," noting that they strived to look perfect on the outside, but their insides—their lack of compassion and kindness—may as well have been a boneyard.

Interestingly, Joan Bunning associates the Four of Pentacles with blocked change and control, which fits perfectly with the words and actions of my former friends and church board.

In his book *The Spiritual Science of the Stars*, Pete Stewart makes the powerful observation that although some have considered the thunderbolt a weapon of God, Zeus actually used it to reduce the world to its original state. It was a symbol of an utter restructuring of the universe. He notes that Buddhist iconography indicates that the thunderbolt was actually a symbol of indestructible enlightenment, a *vajra* signifying the shattering of an illusory reality.

In my case, the bolt hitting the Tower came in the form of a peculiar minister bearing a forbidden secret—one that instantly, quietly disintegrated the ivory towers of theology and my shaky "house built on the sand," as Jesus would say. My eyes were now clear, my understanding finally illuminated in one pivotal instant, and the jumbled puzzle pieces of my relationship with God suddenly assembled into a reasonable picture that finally felt right to me.

The companion booklet to the *Jean Noblet Tarot* echoes my experience perfectly and says this about the Tower: "The multitude of past experience and memories suddenly rearrange themselves into an orderly, meaningful constellation. It is a dazzling experience of fusion with the divine, appropriately named the House of God."

## Your Turn

— Is there something about you that makes you feel or seem different from those around you? Have you ever been ridiculed or shunned because of your beliefs, religion, looks, or orientation? While it may be painful, journaling can often be healing and enlightening when we distance ourselves from the situation. In this spirit, choose cards to represent all the components of your experience, including what you learned from it and where you are right now.

— Do you know of someone who has a secret that could cause them to be humiliated or shunned if someone found out? Select cards to represent the secret, as well as what the person must go through to keep it hidden—and what has happened to them thus far.

— Can you think of a public figure who goes against the status quo, often reaping a backlash of controversy or even hatred? Which cards would you pick to represent their actions or ideology, as well as the reactions of those involved?

# THE SPECIAL GIFT
### Wilma Carroll

I used to entertain at parties, reading palms and Tarot cards. One year I was working at a holiday party for a large music company. The head of the marketing department came over to hear my insights. She was delighted with what I had to tell her.

"What kind of music do you like?" she asked.

"Traditional jazz," I told her.

A few days later, on the day of my birthday, I received five CDs (traditional jazz) from her. What a lovely kindness! I had a very happy birthday.

Deck used: *Rider-Waite Tarot*

**Queen of Wands:** To me, the woman on this card is pleasant looking. You see her face—she can be trusted. The wand she holds is indicative of her entrepreneurial nature. The marketing director was obviously a leader if she headed a department. She demonstrated her good business sense by her generous actions, because the CDs were promoting the artists represented by the company.

**Knight of Cups:** This man is delivering something nice that comes in a cup. I received this gift via mail.

**Six of Cups:** This card shows someone giving the gift of a cup of flowers. The entire picture is pleasant: flowers, cups, and a pretty village. The kindness of giving, the joy of receiving—I chose this card to represent these feelings.

**The Sun:** This is my favorite Tarot card. Look how happy the kid is! Look at the joy, laughter, and sunshine in the picture! I had a very happy birthday, despite it coming the day after Christmas. Usually, no one remembers my birthday because of the holidays, but this marketing director did.

## COMMENTARY

As you can see from Wilma's short and sweet BIT Snapshot, the BIT Method doesn't have to be long and involved. You can practice creating brief BIT Snapshots in a restaurant on a napkin, for example. By "capturing" what you see, then matching it with Tarot cards, you've performed the simple beauty of the BIT Method.

## YOUR TURN

— Have you ever received a gift that was just perfect for you? How did it arrive, who was involved, and what were the emotions surrounding the giving and receiving? Select cards to re-create this scenario.

— Have you ever attended a holiday party with lots of people? Were there any memorable characters, conversations, or situations that you over-heard or witnessed? Which cards would you pick to represent these elements of your BIT Snapshot?

— Think of an event, TV show, movie, or book that involved palmistry, Tarot cards, psychic readings, crystal balls, or other type of divination. Was there anything unusual or surprising about the situation? Choose cards to re-create the scenario.

**THE STAR.**

# *Literature, TV, and Movies*

## CINDERELLA
*Janet Boyer*

When you mention Cinderella, most people think of glass slippers, a pumpkin coach, and a fairy godmother. In the original German folktale, however, none of these is present. In fact, there are some pretty bloody goings-on in the original story.

Although the basic familial structure remains intact—the little girl who loses her mother only to have her wealthy father remarry a nasty woman with two equally odious daughters—the modern version of Cinderella barely resembles the older version. In the classic folktale, the stepmother calls the little unnamed girl "stupid goose," declaring she must earn her bread as a servant and forcing her to wear a drab gray frock. There is no bed in the house for the girl, so she must lie upon the ashes in the hearth. Because of her dirty appearances, her stepmother names her Cinderella.

One day, the father prepares to go on a trip and asks his three daughters what they would like him to bring back for them. The two stepsisters request finery and jewels, while Cinderella makes a simple request: the first branch that touches her father's hat on his way home. Upon his return home, the father gives each of the girls her request; his gift to Cinderella is a hazel bough.

Weeping at the thought of her deceased mother, Cinderella buries the bough on her mother's grave, and it turns into a beautiful tree. Three times a day, Cinderella cries and prays under it. Each time, a white bird flies to the tree, and when Cinderella makes a wish, the bird grants it.

The king of the land declares a three-day festival, and Cinderella longs to attend the ball. The hateful stepmother devises a seemingly impossible task for Cinderella as a condition for attendance: Cinderella has one hour to pick out and clean beans from a barrel of ashes. Cinderella calls upon the birds of the air, which help her with her task, not once, but twice. Although Cinderella succeeds, the stepmother never intended to allow her to go to the festival in the first place, so she offers the excuse that the dirty stepdaughter has no clothes and would embarrass them. As her stepmother and stepsisters go off to the ball, Cinderella runs to the hazel tree to beseech the little white bird, who tosses down to her fine clothes of gold and silver. Now appropriately dressed, Cinderella attends the ball.

At the ball, the prince has eyes only for Cinderella, refusing to dance with any other. Each night he asks to walk her home, yet Cinderella flees—not because of the stroke of midnight (which isn't even mentioned), but probably to shield him from her shameful existence. After the second time, the prince wises up, spreading tar so that her left slipper sticks when she makes a third getaway. Cinderella escapes, but the slipper does not.

Like the saccharine version of this fairy tale, the prince does indeed go to Cinderella's house for a fitting. This is where the story gets a bit gruesome, however. Because the silk slipper doesn't fit the first stepsister, the mother hands her daughter a knife, urging her to hack off her big toe and saying that once she becomes queen, she won't need to walk anyway. Surprisingly, the girl does as she's told, cramming her bloody foot into the delicate slipper. On the carriage ride to the palace, they pass under the hazel tree. The white bird, seeing that the girl's foot is too big and there's blood in the shoe, exclaims, "She's not the bride for you!"

The prince takes her back to the house, and the second stepsister tries on the shoe. This time, the stepmother urges her daughter to slice off her heel instead. The prince and the second stepsister ride under the hazel tree, and the white bird again declares the girl to be the wrong one.

Finally, the prince asks if the family has a third daughter. The shoe fits Cinderella (although why she would want to wear a bloody slipper is beyond me!), and they live happily ever after.

At the end of the story, the two stepsisters are struck blind, but unfortunately, this is the only comeuppance visited upon the cruel family.

Decks used: *Lo Scarabeo Tarot* and *Universal Waite Tarot*

**The Empress:** In the German folktale, Cinderella's mother lies on her deathbed and charges her daughter to be "pious and good" so that "God will always protect you." In addition, she promises to look down from heaven and think of her daughter. I didn't choose the Empress, however, to represent only Cinderella's mother (although this card can indicate a maternal figure). In the *Lo Scarabeo Tarot*, there is a white bird embroidered on the dress of the Empress, right above her pregnant belly. It is a white bird that watches over Cinderella, giving her provisions in her difficult living conditions, so the bird seems to represent a spiritual form of her mother—an angel in disguise.

I've also chosen the Empress to represent the "wicked stepmother." As I mentioned before, each card of the Tarot contains a vast continuum of meanings—from light to dark or unconscious to conscious. Some of the manifestations of the mother archetype include devouring, smothering, abusive, jealous, and neglectful mothers. The stepmother in this story represents the type of cruel parent that fills mythology and, sadly, even modern news reports.

**The Emperor:** The Emperor can be a benign ruler, a brutal dictator, or a loving father figure. For the story of Cinderella, I've chosen the Emperor to do double duty: First, he represents the energy of the father. Second, in the Lo Scarabeo card, there is a bee emblazoned on the Emperor's garment. This symbol reminded me of the emotional sting that Cinderella must have felt when her father failed to protect her from the brutality of his new wife and stepdaughters.

**The Devil:** It would be easy to associate this card with the stepmother because of its association with evil. I chose the Devil from this deck, however, because the image shows two human figures standing before a monstrous figure, which has a second snarling mouth on its stomach. This horrific image reminds me of humanity's cruelty toward humanity. It can be mind-boggling to consider the atrocities that humans have perpetrated upon one another, especially "caretakers" who strip children of dignity, innocence, and a loving home.

**Strength:** With the image of an elegant, feminine woman cradling the open jaws of a lion, this card, to me, represents grace under pressure. Cinderella's lack of complaint and vindictiveness in the face of ridicule and rejection demonstrates her poise, gentle demeanor, and quiet strength.

**The Star:** In the Lo Scarabeo deck, there is an image of a nude woman pouring red liquid onto a lily pad and clear liquid onto a rose. A white bird sits among the flaming branches of a tree under a canopy of stars. The white bird in this card reminds me of the hope that the bird in the story gives to Cinderella. The Star card can also indicate optimism after great calamity.

**Seven of Cups:** The Universal Waite card shows a dizzying array of choices, such as jewels, sandcastles, a dragon, a laurel wreath, a snake, the bust of a man's head, and a cloaked figure, all presented in chalices. We're not told if there are any limits to what Cinderella can ask of the white bird, but she seems to choose simply and intelligently. I see the sevens of Tarot as representing strategy and intelligence. I feel that Cinderella, somewhere deep within, suspected that getting to the ball someway, somehow, was the ticket out of her desperate situation.

**Queen of Cups:** The cups suit often represents intuition, emotion, dreams, and relationships. I view the Queen of Cups as the paragon of emotional intelligence, as well as a highly attuned, even psychic, person who accesses Spirit from deep within when acting and choosing. (This view stems less from how the card looks and more from associations I've made with this card over the years.) Rather than making a materialistic request, Cinderella requests as her present the first branch her father's hat touches, and then she plants the bough on her mother's grave in reverence. Rather than deny her feelings, she is emotionally authentic and grieves outright—watering the hazel branch with her tears. Through her simple request (was it a premonition?) and emotional honesty, a magical conduit for blessing, provision, and comfort sprouts from the earth.

**Four of Wands:** I chose this card to represent the festival thrown by the king. This card often represents celebrations and gatherings, and because this particular image shows a happy couple holding bouquets and bunches of grapes, it reminded me of the fortuitous meeting of Cinderella and the prince.

**Judgement:** In the *Lo Scarabeo Tarot*, this card shows an angel blowing the "last trump" while holding an hourglass. Time is apparently "up" for humanity, and the dead arise out of their graves presumably to be reunited with God. In fundamentalist Christianity, Judgement Day is a time when all wrongs are righted, and the wicked are punished swiftly and justly. Vengeance seems to be an all-too-human trait projected onto a deity, however, perhaps to explain life's injustices, such as those who get away with violence and malice.

In this story, the stepmother and her daughters don't get away with their deception because of a bold bird that sings the truth from a treetop.

It seems to me that the stepdaughters, depending on their age, may have been victims as much as Cinderella was, if their stepmother indoctrinated them. It also seems that the ones truly deserving of punishment are, in fact, the stepmother and Cinderella's father. Ah, but many things are fantastical, surprising, and even unfair in fairy tales, which may be one reason for their universal appeal.

## COMMENTARY

There is a broad range of detail and emotion in most fairy tales, which makes them an ideal source for BIT Snapshots. Cards can be selected to represent people, emotions, thoughts, actions, characteristics, objects, causes, effects, environment, dialogue, archetypal themes, and much more.

Some fairy tales contain elements of sadness, even grief. Although Cinderella certainly feels sorrow at the loss of her mother, I chose not to pick cards for her grief since her story is more about her resourcefulness, grace, and rebirth into a new life. I could have chosen the Three of Swords for her grief or perhaps even the Five of Cups. The Five of Coins (as the suit of pentacles is called in the *Lo Scarabeo Tarot*) could represent her superficial destitution, and Death could symbolize her entrance into a new life. But maybe it's as Joan Bunning said to me after she did her BIT Snapshot: "What you don't choose may be as illuminating as what cards you *do* select."

## YOUR TURN

— Which fairy tales, myths, or superhero stories were—or are—your favorites? Did you ever long to have a magic lamp or fairy godmother to grant you three (or unlimited!) wishes? What would you wish for, and how do you think your life would change if those wishes were fulfilled? Choose cards to represent heroes, villains, outrageous wishes, or the incredible theoretical outcomes of your choices.

— Have you ever witnessed a Good Samaritan in action? Or have you heard about some random act of kindness or benevolent patronage? Which cards would you pick to represent the circumstances?

— Can you think of a book, movie, tale, or real-life occurrence that champions the underdog or centers on someone rescuing or aiding another person (or persons) in a powerful way? What cards seem to speak of the events and characters involved?

# OF MICE AND MEN
### Nina Lee Braden

Very few novels hit readers in the solar plexus, taking their breath away, making them feel shocked and assaulted, but *Of Mice and Men*, by John Steinbeck, is one such book. Published as a novel in 1937, it was produced as a Broadway play the next year and made into a movie in 1939. The setup is simple. During the Great Depression, two migrant farmworkers, George Milton and Lennie Small, travel together, dreaming of one day having a little ranch of their own where Lennie, who likes soft things, can raise rabbits. Lennie is both physically strong and mentally challenged, leading him inadvertently into trouble because he doesn't realize his own strength or its consequences. Time after time, Lennie's behavior forces the twosome to pick up and move. Although George complains a lot about Lennie's stupidity, it is obvious that the little man is very fond of his friend.

At the beginning of the novel, George and Lennie are on their way to the latest in a long line of jobs. Once they are hired, they find two problems. First, the boss's son, Curley, is an aggressive short man who likes to pick fights with men who are bigger than he is. Second, Curley's wife is a pretty, bored, flirtatious woman who singles out Lennie to flirt with.

Not all at the ranch is bad for George and Lennie. They make friends with Candy, an old, one-handed man with an ancient, dying dog. Candy's dog is in great pain, and Candy is talked into letting Carlson (another ranch hand) kill the dog to put him out of his misery. Candy, in his grief, latches on to George and Lennie's dream, asking to be included. He has some money saved up, and with Candy's money, the dream of a little ranch becomes a real possibility. Candy's one regret is that he let someone else kill his dog. He tells George, "I ought to have shot that dog myself, George. I shouldn't ought to of let no stranger shoot my dog."

Fast forward: Lennie is in the barn, playing with his new puppy. He accidentally kills it and is very upset, not so much because he has killed the puppy but because now George won't let him tend the rabbits on their dream ranch. Curley's wife comes in, and the two of them discuss how much they like to touch soft things. She seductively invites him to touch her hair, but when he gets carried away, she starts to scream. Lennie, trying to muffle her screams, accidentally kills her.

The ranch hands, headed up by Curley, form a lynch mob to track and kill Lennie. George, afraid of what will happen when the mob finds Lennie, gets to his friend first. He tells Lennie that he isn't mad and that Lennie can still tend the rabbits. Then George says, "Look there across the river, like you can almost see the place." While Lennie is gazing away, picturing the dream ranch, George shoots him in the back of the head.

In the page remaining of the novel, Slim, the ranch foreman, says to George, "You hadda, George. I swear you hadda." And he takes George away so that they can both get drunk.

This is the point where George would do a Back in Time Snapshot, sitting with Slim in the bunkhouse, half-drunk, dreams shattered, feeling horribly guilty and conflicted, and yet not knowing what else he could have done. Here are George's components and the corresponding Tarot cards.

Decks used: *DruidCraft Tarot, Gill Tarot, Golden Dawn Ritual Tarot, Hanson-Roberts Tarot, Osho Zen Tarot, Renaissance Tarot, Robin Wood Tarot, Sacred Rose Tarot, Thoth Tarot, Voyager Tarot*

**The Fool** and **Strength:** *Lennie.* In the *Golden Dawn Ritual Tarot*, the Fool is pictured a child seated in a garden and curled up with a big white wolf. This picture matches Lennie, the eternal child, at harmony with nature and in the company of a wild animal. He is truly innocent. The Fool does not fully describe Lennie, however. For a complete picture, we need to look at the Strength card from the *Renaissance Tarot*, which shows Hercules wrestling with a lion. Lennie has the strength of Hercules, and his strength is emphasized repeatedly in the story. His childlike mind would not be a problem if he were weak physically, but the combination of a Herculean strength with a child's mind is.

**Knight of Wands:** *Curley.* The *Sacred Rose Tarot* Knight of Wands is truly horrifying. In and of itself, this Knight of Wands is not necessarily violent. Anger and action are always just beneath his surface, however. As Curley goes off to hunt Lennie, he rides a horse, like the knight, and carries a rifle in place of a wand. You don't want the Knight of Wands mad at you, but no matter how Lennie tried to avoid a fight, Curley was determined to pick one.

**Lust:** *Curley's wife.* Curley's wife is given no name in *Of Mice and Men*. She exists in the story primarily as a temptation to the ranch hands. She is filled with unfulfilled longing. Surely, Lust from the Thoth deck is the perfect card for Curley's wife.

**Knight of Pentacles:** *Slim.* Slim is the head ranch hand. He doesn't own the ranch, but he is the center of it. He is steady and masterful, holding everything together. Almost any deck's Knight of Pentacles would fit Slim, but the Prince of Coins, the *Gill Tarot*'s equivalent of this knight, and its keyword "construction" seem particularly apt. The prince stands in front of a path winding to a mountain, holding a huge wagon wheel.

**The Hermit:** *Candy.* Many mythic tales have an old wise man who gives a gift to the hero. In Tarot, the old wise man is the Hermit. Candy gives his money to George and Lennie and offers his wisdom to George. For Candy, the Hermit from the *DruidCraft Tarot* seems particularly appropriate, since the card shows an old man accompanied by a wolf, which the deck's authors associate with inner wisdom.

**Ten of Cups:** *The dream ranch.* The Hanson-Roberts deck, with its gentle and soft pictures, is the perfect place to find a card for George and Lennie's dream ranch. I call the Ten of Cups the "happy family card" or the "poor but happy card" or even sometimes the *Little House on the Prairie* card, and these associations are visually personified in the Hanson-Roberts deck. All three phrases fit the dream ranch, which, unfortunately, did not become a reality.

**The Tower:** *Shooting Lennie.* In the *Voyager Tarot*'s Tower, the image shows leaves and flowers, suggesting Lennie's woodland death. Also, one of the figures is deliberately diving from the tower, suggesting George's deliberate action.

**Three of Clouds:** *George.* Although we may not agree with his choice, we know that George acted from love and good intentions. George is certainly heartbroken by his action. No matter how noble, generous, or selfless his action, however, he still killed his best friend. He will live with that pain and sorrow for the rest of his life. The Three of Clouds from the *Osho Zen Tarot* (the equivalent of the Three of Swords) with its keyword "ice-olation," seems particularly apt. In this card, a figure stands frozen in ice, and only his tears can move.

I would like to think that George eventually heals, and that one day he is able to have a little ranch of his own. Realistically, George will probably live a relatively short life, filled with grief and guilt. Although I have chosen all of the cards deliberately thus far, let me shuffle and deal one card, just for George. Let's call it a card of hope.

Amazingly, I have drawn the Lovers from the *Robin Wood Tarot*. There is hope for George, and I am somewhat comforted.

## COMMENTARY

Not only can you create a BIT Snapshot for any work of literature, but you can also get inside the head of a character and choose "what if" cards for a character, as Nina Lee did for George. In fact, I have a spin on the BIT Method called retro-divination, where cards are selected facedown, at random, rather than consciously. You formulate the components of your snapshot using the BIT Method, but leave it up to the Universe to select the cards for you. In this way, you can gather insight about any circumstance that troubles, intrigues, or confuses you—a commentary from the gods, so to speak.

The *Robin Wood Tarot*'s Lovers card is a loving picture of a youthful female and male tenderly embracing while an angel peers from behind a cloud as if to bestow comfort or peace upon them, so I can see why Nina Lee felt a sense of hope when choosing this card.

In the Thoth deck, Crowley names Trump 11 "Lust." In Rider-Waite–style decks, this card is often known as Strength. About the Lust card, Crowley expert Lon Milo DuQuette has this to say in his book *Understanding Aleister*

*Crowley's Thoth Tarot:* "The principal deities connected with this card are those who, by tradition, are associated with the power of the female to arouse, harness, and direct the animal nature . . ."

In the *Sacred Rose Tarot*, both the rider and the horse in this blood-red card bear matching menacing stares from white, sightless eyes. Deck creator and artist Johanna Gargiulo-Sherman says of this image: "Out of a fiery landscape a knight charges toward us, his horse wearing on its forehead the emblem of fire, the red triangle . . . This card signifies an impetuous person—unpredictable, active, alert, with a very sensual nature. There is a need to act quickly, without warning."

## YOUR TURN

— Have you ever been faced with a "darned if you do, darned if you don't" type of situation? What did you do? Choose cards to illustrate your dilemma, as well as your thoughts and the ramifications of your choices.

— Do you know of someone who has a combination of personality traits that seem like a recipe for disaster? What cards seem to symbolize the various traits, as well as the type of circumstances that individual has experienced? Alternatively, do a theoretical BIT Snapshot based on a fictitious situation that such a person might encounter.

— Recall a situation from literature, history, or popular culture in which someone faced temptation. Which cards would you select to represent the components of this scenario?

# MARY POPPINS

*Janet Boyer*

Supercalifragilisticexpialidocious—that's what you say when you don't know *what* to say. At least, that's what a magical flying nanny asserts.

Released in 1964, the fanciful movie *Mary Poppins* heralded Julie Andrews's film debut, and her portrayal of Mary won her an Academy Award for best actress. Dick Van Dyke played her on-screen sidekick, a Cockney-accented chimney sweep named Bert. The movie was based on the 1934 novel by P. L. Travers.

At the start of the movie, Mary sits atop a carpetbag perched on a cloud, powdering her nose, a folded umbrella at her side. We soon find out what she's waiting for.

Seventeen Cherry Tree Lane is home of George Banks, Esq.; his wife, Winifred; and his children, Jane and Michael. Chaos has broken out, because Katie Nanna, the nanny, has finally decided to quit. Jane and Michael have run away for the fourth time in a week, and she's fed up with their shenanigans. Because Mrs. Banks has hired six nannies, all of whom have been disasters, Mr. Banks takes it upon himself to put an advertisement in the paper. In his opinion, he feels the new nanny should govern the children just like he does the bank where he works: with precision.

Eventually found at the zoo by a constable, the runaway children come into the room with their *own* requirements for a nanny, reciting them to their father through song. Irritated, Mr. Banks sends Jane and Michael to the nursery, tearing up their list of preferences and tossing the bits of paper into the fireplace.

The next morning there is a queue of nannies at the door. The children look out the second-story window and Jane sadly observes, "I don't understand. They're not what we advertised for at all." Just then, a strong wind arrives, blowing away the applicants. Mary Poppins comes floating down via her opened umbrella and is the only applicant standing at the door when Mr. Banks opens it. She briskly walks into the house, and when asked by Mr. Banks for her references, she replies that references are "a very old-fashioned idea." She pulls out an ad and reads its requirements back to Mr. Banks, but it's not *his* ad she's holding; it's the list the children wrote, mysteriously reassembled. Mary then takes immediate charge of the children, and Mr. and Mrs. Banks excitedly agree that she'll be firm, give commands, and mold them.

It's immediately apparent to Jane and Michael that Mary Poppins isn't an ordinary nanny. Out of her carpetbag, she pulls a hat stand, a wall mirror, a tall plant, and a lamp. Mary responds to the children's incredulity by saying, "Never judge things by their appearance. Not even carpetbags. I'm sure I never do."

She notices that the nursery is in disarray and suggests a game of "well begun is half done." This translates as "let's tidy up the nursery." Michael says to his sister, "I told you she was tricky." Jane asks the new nanny, "It *is* a game, isn't it, Mary Poppins?" Mary replies, "Well, it depends on your point of view. You see, in every job that must be done, there is an element of fun. You find the fun, and snap! The job's a game."

Although Mary Poppins acts as though the odd situations she originates are completely normal, it's obvious to most everyone else that they're anything *but.*

While Mary and the children are on their way to the park for an outing, they run into Bert, the chimney sweep. Bert, an old friend of Mary's, is in the middle of making one of his sidewalk chalk drawings. He says to them, "Other nannies take children to the park. When you're with Mary Poppins, suddenly you're in places you've never dreamed of." Bert tells the children that they can enter in any of the worlds that the chalk drawings portray. He appeals to Mary to make it happen, but she replies dismissively, "I have no intention of making a spectacle of myself, thank you."

After Bert's failed attempt to enter one of the chalk drawings, Mary resignedly transports them into one that depicts a fair in the countryside. "Control yourself!" she exclaims to them, as if there is some propriety to even the surreal situations in which they find themselves.

Mary and Bert dance and dine with penguins while the children are off playing. Then they all meet up at the carousel. The carousel horses break free, and off they all go for a leisurely ride, a foxhunt, and then a horse race. Practically perfect Mary wins the race, but as they are celebrating and singing "Supercalifragilisticexpialidocious," it begins to rain, smudging the sidewalk painting's chalk and returning them to the "real" world.

Back at their home, the children beg Mary to stay as their nanny. She says that she'll stay just until the wind changes. The children excitedly review the day's events, but Mary denies that she was ever in a horse race: "A respectable person like me in a horse race? How dare you suggest such a thing!" The children object, and Michael exclaims, "But I saw you do it!" Mary ignores their protests and tells them to go to sleep.

The next day, Mary, Bert, and the children visit Mary's ailing Uncle Albert, who is suffering from a strange malady: whenever he laughs, he floats up to the ceiling. It turns out that his malady is contagious; that is, when other people in his house laugh, they, too, begin to float. The group ends up having tea—on the ceiling!

Upon returning home, Mary suggests to Mr. Banks that the children accompany him to work, so they might learn how to "walk the straight and narrow with pride." Mr. Banks concurs, thinking that it's a wonderful idea.

When Mary goes upstairs to the nursery to tell them of the planned outing, Jane exclaims that when they go to the city, their father can point out the sights. Mary solemnly replies, "Well, most things he can. Sometimes those we love, through no fault of their own, can't see past the end of his nose."

The following day, Mr. Banks and the children walk together toward the bank. Michael has a tuppence to spend, and when he notices an old woman selling small bags of food to feed the birds, he decides he'd like to spend his money on one. Mr. Banks thinks this purchase is ridiculous and steers the children sharply toward the bank. While there, Michael refuses to invest his tuppence in the bank (despite insistent prodding by the bank founder and other trustees), and his raucous outcry causes a run on the bank.

Back at the Banks home, a downtrodden Mr. Banks laments to Bert (who is at the house to clean the chimney), "You know what I think? It's that woman Mary Poppins! From the moment she stepped into this house, things began to happen to me. . . . My world was calm, well ordered, exemplary. Then came this person with chaos in her wake. And now my life's ambitions go, with one fell blow. It's quite a bitter pill to take."

Bert attempts to explain Mary's unique way of looking at things, and George exclaims, "That's exactly what I mean! Changing bread and water into tea and cakes, indeed! . . . No wonder everything's higgledy-piggledy here!" Bert acts sympathetic, assuring him that an important person like himself is understandably too busy to dry the children's tears or look into their smiling, grateful faces. Bert begins to sing, "You've got to grind, grind, grind at that grindstone. Though childhood slips like sand through a sieve. And all too soon they've up and grown, and then they've flown, and it's too late for you to give . . . just that spoonful of sugar to help the medicine go down."

Soon after, Mr. Banks gets a call from the other bankers in the firm telling him to come to the bank at once. While there, they fire him, blaming him for Michael's outburst that caused the run on the bank. Something comes over

Mr. Banks, and he repeats a joke he heard from Michael (a joke that he not only didn't get earlier, but that he also scoffed at). He laughs freely and unashamedly, as if he has a new lease on life. He shouts, "Mary Poppins was *right!*"

Mr. Banks arrives home disheveled but jubilant. He then picks up his wife and spins her around while singing, as the housemaids look on in disbelief.

The wind changes direction, and Mary Poppins is packing her things. Michael comments sadly, "She doesn't care what happens to us." Jane answers, "She only promised to stay 'til the wind changed . . . Mary Poppins, don't you love us?" Mary says, "And what would happen to me, may I ask, if I loved all the children I say good-bye to?"

The children go downstairs and, to their surprise, Mr. Banks has fixed Michael's broken kite. Michael asks, "However did you manage it?" Mr. Banks replies, "With tuppence for paper and strings, you can have your own set of wings." A big difference from his earlier attitude toward the tuppence he was trying to force Michael to invest!

Mary looks out the window to see the family skipping down the sidewalk to go fly their kite in the park. Mr. Banks gets his job back and gains a new respect and appreciation for his life and family.

Just like that spoonful of sugar, Mary Poppins delivered her own brand of "medicine"; and when it ran its course, perspectives shifted, appreciation flourished, and a family learned what was really important in life.

Deck used: *Universal Waite Tarot*

This BIT Snapshot will be a bit different. Rather than consciously pairing cards with the actions and nuances of the movie Mary Poppins, I'm going to select some of my favorite quotes from the movie and create a BIT Snapshot based on them. In the "Your Turn" exercise, however, *you* will be pairing cards with the elements from the movie. Even if you haven't seen it, I've provided enough details for you to construct a BIT Snapshot.

**Judgement:** *"But I feel what's to happen, all happened before."* In the beginning of the movie, Bert is wearing a contraption fitted with various instruments, and he entertains a crowd on the sidewalk with musical medleys. He then begins to do some lyrical improvisation about the various people in the crowd whom he knows. Just as he's ready to sing a song about Miss Persimmon, leaves begin to swirl. Losing his train of thought, Bert looks around, comments about the east wind and the "mist moving in, like somethin' is brewing . . . about to begin." When I have that odd feeling of déjà vu, I often say this quote from Bert (complete with the Cockney accent!) and wonder if I'm experiencing a mile marker I set up for myself pre-incarnation.

According to some authors, this unusual sensation that we sometimes experience may very well be a "mile marker" that we have set up with our "life selection coordinators" before incarnating. Based on data collected from hundreds of patients, Michael Newton, in the books *Journey of Souls* and *Destiny of Souls*, catalogues past-life regressions that detail what happens between lives. Theoretically, we view potential lives before incarnating to consider if they would fit the needs of our soul growth. We then program certain markers into our souls, which will jog our memory about our objectives—why we came to Earth in the first place.

Although the Judgement card often depicts the Christian idea of a last judgement, I tend to associate this card with past-life issues and pre-incarnation agreements. In keeping with Newton's books, I believe that we structure our life lessons and experience; and after death, with our soul guides and a council of elders, we decide if we met our self-scripted challenges satisfactorily or need to reflect on further growth.

**Justice:** *"Never judge things by appearances . . . I never do."* Whether intentional or not, this phrase is almost a direct quote from Jesus. In the New Testament book of John, the religious leaders were angry with Jesus because he healed a man on the Sabbath, thus breaking Mosaic law. Jesus finds this assertion unbelievable: "Do not judge according to appearances, but judge with righteous judgement" (7:24). In the New Testament, there's a phrase saying that the letter of the law "kills," but the spirit of the law "gives life." While Jesus broke the letter of the law—the literal decree prohibiting work on the Sabbath—he certainly kept with the spirit of the law.

The woman pictured in the Justice card holds a sword in one hand and a set of scales in the other. She is not blindfolded, but sees everything. Symbolically, I see the scales as an image of "weighing the heart"—not judging by appearances or the adherence of any external laws, but rather seeing with the eyes of the heart. Just as the children "judged" that mere carpetbags couldn't hold hat stands and wall mirrors, Mary proved that mind-boggling "magic" can and does happen amid quite ordinary circumstances. Likewise, Jesus encouraged humanity not to judge fellow humans based on appearance, but to discern with the heart and thus remain open to the seemingly miraculous.

**Nine of Pentacles:** *"I does what I likes, and I likes what I do."* As Bert draws various chalk scenes on the sidewalk, he sings this phrase during the rousing tune "Chim Chim Cher-ee," which segues into a full-blown dance routine. When I see the self-assured woman displayed on this card in most Rider-Waite–inspired decks, I envision a woman who knows herself well, one who is comfortable in her own skin and enjoys life to the fullest, no matter her station in life. Although Bert observes that some may regard a chimney sweep as the "bottom rung on the ladder," he counters, "there's no happier bloke" than he. Completely in the moment, trusting everything, and prohibiting nothing (like Bert!), the woman in the Nine of Pentacles is to me one who is content to live and let live. She doesn't force ill-fitting circumstances to bend to her preferences because she is flexible and adaptive.

**The Devil:** *"I love to laugh."* Barely able to contain himself, Uncle Albert sings the song "I Love to Laugh" while floating in the air, inserting a smattering of corny jokes between guffaws. Of course, Bert can't control himself, and neither can the children, so as they float upward, the seemingly uptight Mary Poppins has no choice but to join them for tea on the ceiling.

The Devil may seem a very odd choice for the light-hearted phrase "I love to laugh," but it just so happens that in the esoteric Qabalistic tradition (a mystical offshoot of Judaism), adherents assign the quality of laughter to this card. In his classic book *The Tarot: A Key to the Wisdom of the Ages*, world-renowned Tarot and Qabalah authority Paul Foster Case writes of Key 15, the Devil: *"Mirth*, the function of consciousness attributed by Qabalists to the [Hebrew] letter *Ayin*, is usually provoked by incongruity, by human weaknesses, foibles, and shortcomings. Nevertheless, laughter is prophylactic. It purifies subconsciousness and dissolves mental complexes and conflicts."

For centuries, the figment of the devil has been used by religion to scare the figurative hell out of people, instilling a sense of guilt, fear, and rigidity. If the Hierophant pushes his sense of morality on the masses, then it's the Devil who thumbs his nose at propriety, including introducing hearty laughter to a proper high tea, if need be.

**The Emperor:** *"Give it back! Give it back!"* When at the bank, everyone pressures Michael to relinquish his tuppence for investment. Michael screams this phrase, which is what causes a panic among the bank customers. Although the bank is an institution that could be a part of the Emperor's domain, I chose this card to represent Michael's ability to set boundaries for himself, to be the Emperor of his own life.

**Knight of Pentacles:** *"Sometimes those we love, through no fault of their own, can't see past the end of his nose."* In the *Universal Waite Tarot*, this knight is the only one portrayed as standing completely still. Some might consider him stodgy, even boring. (After all, a knight standing still, appearing almost leaden, is unlikely to be on a quest of any kind, let alone one filled with adventure.) Like the Knight of Pentacles, George Banks was reliable in his work duties, to the point of bringing his work home. When he did interact with Jane and Michael, he treated them more like money—something to be managed—rather than children. Because the Knight of Pentacles could be viewed as quite stubborn, much like Mr. Banks, he may have to experience a thunderous wake-up call to knock him off his horse.

## COMMENTARY

As mentioned before, the suit of pentacles is usually associated with the element of earth, as well as the astrological earth signs of Taurus, Virgo, and Capricorn. On one end of the spectrum, earth energy is grounding, reliable, meticulous, and practical. On the other end, earth energy can be stagnant, resistant to change, materialistic, and overly concerned with self-preservation. So when I think of this kind of solid earth energy coupled with what seems to be a fiery, energetic knight energy, I see a plow horse rather than a racehorse. Nothing wrong with that, of course—not every-one can be a daring knight at best or a Don Quixote at worst!

Although the King of Pentacles might be a reasonable choice to pair with Mr. Banks, I tend to see the kings as ones who exhibit the energy of their suit in a more extroverted or controlling way. Just as I happen to view the King of Pentacles as the "Donald Trump card," so I would view the actual owner of the film's Fidelity Fiduciary Bank—or even the entire board who helped decide the fate of Mr. Banks—as the King of Pentacles. In other words, the Knight of Pentacles is more a cog in a wheel rather than one who controls the machine.

The *Osho Zen Tarot* features expressive artwork and Zen-inspired wisdom. The deck's companion book calls the Nine of Rainbows card (the equivalent of the Nine of Pentacles) Ripeness, saying, "That moment is really of great bliss—when there is no seeking, no longing, no desire, nowhere to go, nothing to achieve. One has come home; one has attained relaxation. One is in immense rest . . . not even a ripple in the mind. In that very state god happens."

In addition to the two Newton books mentioned, other books that address the theory of pre-incarnation agreements we make about our upcoming life in accordance to what our souls desire to experience and learn in the next go-around are *Courageous Souls*, by Robert Schwartz; *Sacred Contracts*, by Caroline Myss; and *Transforming Fate into Destiny*, by Robert Ohotto.

## YOUR TURN

— Has there ever been a time when you just threw up your hands and said, "Oh, what the hell"—giving in to a person, circumstance, or attitude that originally felt like an obstruction or perhaps even an unsavory notion? What precipitated your giving in, and what happened when you changed course? Choose cards to reflect your experience.

— Think of a time when you witnessed a dysfunctional family or perhaps an unruly child or group of children. Which cards remind you of the individuals and the craziness that ensued?

— Pick out certain elements from the movie *Mary Poppins* and create a BIT Snapshot. Remember, there's no wrong way to do the BIT Method, so be as brief or as elaborate as you'd like—and have fun with the process!

# The Little Match Girl

*Janet Boyer*

A heartbreaking tale by beloved author Hans Christian Andersen, "The Little Match Girl" chronicles the last day of an abused, impoverished little girl forced to sell matchsticks in the bitter cold. Barefoot and freezing, she walks the streets, dodging carriages as the smell of roast goose and other delicious foods wafts from brightly lit windows. It is New Year's Eve, and although she briefly considers going home, she remembers that if she does so she will incur a beating because she hasn't sold any matchsticks that evening.

Curling up on the stoop of a recessed house, the little girl lights one of the matches to warm herself. To her delight, she sees a vision of a blazing, warming fire in a brass stove—only the vision vanishes when the match goes out.

When she strikes another match, a beautifully set table laden with food appears before her. But, as with the last match, the vision dissipates with the flame. When she strikes a third match, she sees the grandest Christmas tree, with thousands of candles twinkling among its branches. The candles seem to reach to the heavens, until they turn into stars. She notices that one of the stars is falling, streaking across the sky.

"Someone is dying," she thinks, for her deceased grandmother once said to her that when a star falls, it is a soul making its way back to God. As she lights the last match, she sees her gentle, happy grandmother. Knowing that her grandmother will disappear when the light goes out, the little girl hastily lights the rest of the matches, begging grandmother to take her with her.

The grandmother gathers the girl in her arms, and they ascend far above the earth. There is no more hunger, pain, or cold, because they are now both with God.

The next day, townspeople find the little girl frozen to death, spent matches clutched in her hand and a smile on her face.

Deck used: *Universal Waite Tarot*

**Five of Pentacles:** Many decks in the Rider-Waite tradition show two figures huddling under lighted windows in the snow. This card perfectly captures many aspects of the "Little Match Girl," including the little girl's poverty and environment.

**The High Priestess:** I chose this card to represent the little match girl's grandmother. In the companion booklet to the *Jean Noblet Tarot*, reproduced by French artisan Jean-Claude Flornoy, this card (known as the Papess in the Tarot de Marseille tradition) represents grandmothers. The author of the companion booklet writes, "The Papess is the grandmother: the first adult encountered by the infant. In medieval society, it is not the mother, but the grandmother, who has charge of the children's education until the age of five . . . [T]he very small child first sees the world through the eyes of his grandmother." Through example and perhaps overt tutelage, the little girl's grandmother influenced the girl's perspective so that it included resilience, optimism, and faith.

**Ten of Pentacles:** Wealth, fine food, and celebrating families surrounded the little girl on New Year's Eve—a scenario I connect with this card because of the abundance of coins in the Ten of Pentacles, as well as what appears in the imagery to be family members from three generations.

**Ten of Swords:** The little girl was literally left out in the cold by townsfolk. At the beginning of the story, one boy even steals her slipper, saying that it would make a good cradle when he grows up to have a child of his own. Although consciously neglected, even ridiculed, she focuses on a spiritual sunrise that occurs within. While the figure in the foreground shows a man lying facedown with swords in his back, I see the sunrise in the background of the Universal Waite image for this card representing her internal "spiritual sunrise."

**Ten of Cups:** When discussing several case histories of clients with full-blown AIDS who later died, author Ly de Angeles notes that the Ten of Cups often came up in the Outcome position of the Celtic Cross spread for these individuals. Life is akin to hopscotch, she notes in her book *Tarot Theory & Practice*, "a seeming obstacle course, dependent sometimes on skill, sometimes on seeming fate, to get the participant to Home where they are safe and have completed the game." Given de Angeles's assertion that the "bottom-line interpretation of that card is *home*," the Ten of Cups seems a perfect summation of the little girl's final earthly minutes and her transition to the other side, to be with God and her beloved grandmother.

## COMMENTARY

Had this tale spun a different way, with the girl begging for help or kind strangers reaching out to her, I might have picked the Six of Pentacles, which shows someone of financial means helping the poor. I tend to see that card as two sides of the same coin: the beggar and the philanthropist. In the *Wheel of Change Tarot*, by Alexandra Genetti, the Six of Disks shows small pools of blood on top of coins and paper, which could be a fitting image for suffering (and dying) in the midst of great wealth.

Because the townsfolk passed by the barefoot girl, and one boy even taunted her and stole her only shoe, the miser of the Four of Pentacles could have been a candidate for this particular BIT Snapshot. I tend to see the Four of Pentacles, however, as hoarding money and goods because of a scarcity mindset and fear of loss more than outright snubbing a suffering individual.

In Tarot numerology, the tens of the Minor Arcana often indicate an abundance of a particular suit. In the *Lo Scarabeo Tarot*, the traveling figure depicted on the Ten of Wands carries ten smoking sticks, whose fires have apparently gone out. While this image would also be appropriate, considering that the dying little girl used up all the matches in order to cling to her wondrous visions (and because her father had shouldered her with the unimaginable responsibility of bringing in income), this card speaks to me of burnout or weariness. Although the little girl was physically uncomfortable, I see Andersen's tale focusing more on her inner resourcefulness and hope rather than fatigue or hardship.

The Celtic Cross spread mentioned by Ly de Angeles is rather popular, especially in old-school Tarot circles. This complex spread usually contains eleven or so cards (depending on the version), addressing these issues:

- You
- What surrounds you
- What blocks you
- Your foundation
- What is behind you
- What crowns you
- What is before you
- Your persona
- How others see you
- Your hopes and fears

The outcome of the situation

If you'd like to know more about the Celtic Cross spread, the *Instant Tarot Reader*, by Monte Farber and Amy Zerner, is an excellent book-and-deck set that supplies meanings for each of the seventy-eight cards in the Tarot in all eleven positions of the spread.

## YOUR TURN

— Have you ever been inspired or comforted by a friend or relative's example or advice? Choose cards that remind you of what you felt or the timely suggestion, as well as how you may have changed as a result.

— Has there been a situation in which you witnessed thoughtlessness or indifference? Which cards would you pick to represent the circumstance?

— Think of a world event or time in history when one or more parties felt a sense of unfairness or injustice. Select cards to represent the era, people, actions, responses, and result.

# MAEVE: THE CELTIC MARY MAGDALEN
### *Elizabeth Cunningham*

Feisty, funny, outspoken, passionate, Maeve is lover, bard, healer, priestess—and no one's disciple. Since 1991, I have been writing her story in a series of novels called the Maeve Chronicles.

The Maeve Chronicles recount the life adventures of an unconventional Mary Magdalen, a redheaded Celt named Maeve. Each novel is designed to stand alone, and the series can be read in any sequence.

*Magdalen Rising*, set at a druid college, tells the tale of Maeve's youthful passion for a student from Galilee known to the Celts as Esus (Jesus). The lovers are forced to part when Maeve defies the authority of the druids to save Jesus' life. *The Passion of Mary Magdalen* follows Maeve's perilous search for Jesus through slavery and prostitution in Rome to founding her own holy whorehouse in Magdala. The ultimate reunion of Maeve and Jesus is as stormy as it is ecstatic, infusing this passionate narrative with their passion for each other. In the end, they dare together the greatest mystery of all. *Bright Dark Madonna*, the third book in the series, is forthcoming from

Monkfish Publishing in spring 2009. *Black-Robed Priestess*, the fourth and concluding chronicle, is in progress.

The BIT Snapshot that follows refers to events in *Magdalen Rising* and *The Passion of Mary Magdalen*. (My thanks to Cait Johnson for her help with this BIT Snapshot.)

Decks used: *Celtic Wisdom Tarot, Llewellyn Tarot, Morgan-Greer Tarot, Motherpeace Tarot, Thoth Tarot*

**Strength** *(Motherpeace Tarot)*: From the outset, I recognized Maeve in the *Motherpeace Tarot* card Strength. Naked and redheaded, the woman of Strength sits under a full moon between a sacred tree and a holy well, surrounded by creatures of the air, the earth, and the water. She holds what appears to be the sun in her hand. A perfect emblem for Maeve, whose compassion and power come from her connection with all creation.

I am now completing *Bright Dark Madonna*, the third volume of the Maeve Chronicles. A few years ago, when I was near completion of the central novel, *The Passion of Mary Magdalen* (now happily published), I contemplated the years and years I'd spent writing that book and its prequel *Magdalen Rising*. I asked myself: What is the essence of the story so far? What if I could tell it in a few lines instead of hundreds of pages? Here is the poem that came as an answer; Tarot cards for each line follow.


    Every birth is a miracle.

    Love is mystery seeking form.

    Trouble follows.

    Loss lasts a long time.

    Reunion is a prelude to more

    Trouble and loss.

Death is love seeking mystery

And then there is only mystery.

In the end, I live for the dawn.


**Ten of Discs** *(Motherpeace Tarot)*: *Every birth is a miracle.* A woman gives birth in a sacred circle. Three women attend her, and the others surround her with shields bearing potent images. In *Magdalen Rising,* Maeve is born to eight warrior witches on an island in the Celtic Otherworld. She refers to them all as "her mothers." Strong communities of women—witches, whores, priestesses, pirates—are an enduring source of sustenance for Maeve.

**The High Priestess** *(Thoth Tarot)*: *Love is mystery seeking form.* The High Priestess sits enthroned behind what looks to me like a fishing net or it could be "the veil between the worlds." She wears the crown of an Egyptian goddess, Isis or Hathor. In her arms, she holds the winds; the seas swirl in her lap. In front of the fishnet veil is the manifest world: crystals, flowers, fruits, and an animal. Maeve declares that she loves Jesus from "before and beyond time in all the worlds." She first glimpses him in the waters of a holy well on her mothers' island. The High Priestess card captures the eternal, between-the-worlds dimension of Maeve's passion for her beloved. Much later in the story, in her own moment of apotheosis, Maeve becomes the goddess Isis incarnate.

**The Changer** *(Celtic Wisdom Tarot)*: *Trouble follows.* In this Celtic version of the Tower card, the spiral in the belly of a stormy god sends branches spinning, overturning cups and human lives. The sky blooms with flowers, wheels, and whirlwinds; the mood is both ominous and exciting. Maeve moves from her natal island, and her dreams of a cosmic love turn into the chaos of incarnate love with Esus, a fellow student at the druid college on Mona. Like any lovers, the pair must contend with culture clash, clashing wills, mixed signals, and missed cues. But their spats pale in comparison to the forces that are massing against them. Over their human lives looms the implacable Changer with the lightning bolt in his hand.

**Six of Swords** *(Llewellyn Tarot): Loss lasts a long time.* Two figures sit huddled together in the middle of a boat, six swords in front of them and a carved angel in the prow. Behind them, a third figure poles the boat into the mist. The mood is one of desolation and exile. When Maeve defies the entire druid college to save the life of her beloved, she is "sent beyond the ninth wave" in a boat without sail or oar. But this exile is nothing compared to the loss of her beloved. The swords in the boat also evoke for me the bitter constraint this headstrong free spirit must confront when she is later captured and sold as a slave in Rome. This encounter with loss and limitation tests and ultimately deepens her spirit, preparing her for what is to come.

**Cernunnos** *(DruidCraft Tarot): Reunion is a prelude to more trouble and loss.* The lovers lie spent in the greenwood. Behind them looms the shadowy figure of Cernunnos, the Celtic horned god, which Christians later identified, however mistakenly, with the devil. In Tarot numerology, the Devil card is connected with the Lovers card. As Trump 15, the number of the Devil reduces to the Lovers' Trump 6.

NOTE FROM JANET: In Tarot numerology, double-digit numbers reduce to single digits. Thus, any Major Arcana card, or trump, numbering 10 through 21 reduces and connects to its single-digit counterpart in some way. The Devil is Trump 15. Because $1 + 5 = 6$, the Devil's corresponding card is Trump 6, the Lovers, the sixth card in the Major Arcana.

This card evokes that mysterious link. The reunion of Maeve and Jesus is poignant, powerful, and all too brief. Both sense that they stand on the brink of some tragedy and/or transformation, a fate that is both chosen and inexorable. The card contains all these paradoxes: free will and destiny, love and danger, death and fecundity.

**Death** *(Morgan-Greer Tarot)*: *Death is love seeking mystery.* A serene death figure, a purple-hooded skull with gold ornament at the throat, stands with the archetypal scythe. In the background, sharp black mountains rise over a red river into a red sky. But it is the foreground that holds my attention: a lush white-yellow rose complete with a thorny green stem. Maeve, like many goddesses of love, is associated with the rose, an anagram of Eros and an ancient metaphor for the folds of a woman's sex organs. When her beloved confronts the mystery of death, Maeve must surrender to the mystery of the rose.

**The Hanged One** *(Motherpeace Tarot)*: *And then there is only mystery.* The woman with the shining hair hangs from a swamp tree, her foot bound to the branch by what looks like the same purple snake that appears in the Motherpeace Strength card. The moon is full; the roots of the trees disappear into water that seamlessly meets the sky. Everything is suspended in that mysterious moment between in breath and out, life and death. In the garden of resurrection, Jesus cautions Maeve before she goes to meet the others: "Explanations are not always a good idea." Explanation too easily becomes dogma and doctrine, articles of faith rather than faith itself. Maeve is a storyteller. A good storyteller leaves mystery intact, inviting "willing suspension of disbelief."

**The Star** *(Llewellyn Tarot)*: *In the end, I live for the dawn.* A red-haired woman sits on the rock by a sacred spring, lifting her face and her right palm to the morning star; her left hand rests over her heart. Behind her is a hill topped with standing stones. The horizon pales with dawn light; an owl wings its way home. Or maybe it is a dove, a bird associated with the goddess Venus, or the planet we call the morning and evening star. In the course of her life, Maeve endures more than one dark night of the soul, as do we all. The morning star is an image not only of the resurrection, but also of the grace and beauty of all risings—hers and ours. In this card, Maeve is both the woman greeting the dawn and the star itself, the shining emblem of love that is stronger than death.

## COMMENTARY

Reflecting woman-centric spirituality, the *Motherpeace Tarot*, by Vicki Noble and Karen Vogel, is quite unusual in that it is one of the only decks with round cards.

The *DruidCraft Tarot*, by Philip and Stephanie Carr-Gomm, illustrated by Will Worthington, is a stunning deck dedicated to the earth-based spirituality of druidism. Like many deck creators, they have changed the names of some cards, substituting the Lady for the Empress, the Lord for the Emperor, Fferyllt for Temperance, Cernunnos for the Devil, and Rebirth for Judgement.

## YOUR TURN

— Elizabeth associates the card Strength with the heroine of her novels. Contemplate someone you would consider a personal hero or heroine. Why do you esteem this person? What traits does he or she exemplify? Select cards to symbolize this individual, as well as his/her actions and character.

— Elizabeth describes Maeve as "feisty, funny, outspoken, passionate." Think of someone you know, or have observed, that embodies those qualities. Which cards would you choose to represent that person, as well as his/her personality traits?

— Consider a favorite or known poem. Alternatively, consult a book of poetry or look up poems online. Some poets with compelling imagery include Robert Frost, Emily Dickinson, e. e. cummings, Maya Angelou, Dylan Thomas, T. S. Eliot, Walt Whitman, Carl Sandburg, Edgar Allan Poe, Rainer Maria Rilke, Rumi, and William Butler Yeats. Select a poem, go through the Tarot, and choose cards that you feel reflect the mood or intent of the various lines. You could choose a card for each line, as Elizabeth did, or pick a card (or cards) to represent stanzas of the poem.

# It's the Great Pumpkin, Charlie Brown!
### *Janet Boyer*

The Halloween season augurs one of the most beloved animated TV shows, four decades running: *It's the Great Pumpkin, Charlie Brown!* An annual viewing tradition for many, this holiday tale from cartoonist Charles M. Schulz chronicles the antics of the gang from his popular comic strip, *Peanuts.*

Charlie Brown; his sister, Sally; friends Linus Van Pelt, Lucy Van Pelt, Pig Pen, and Schroeder; and his dog, Snoopy, all make appearances, but this particular story centers on Linus's fervent expectation of the Great Pumpkin. With an almost religious belief, Linus reverently speaks of the Great Pumpkin, informing all who listen that this benevolent being flies around delivering toys to the "most sincere" pumpkin patch.

Linus defends his ardor to a skeptical Charlie Brown (who notes that the Great Pumpkin sounds a lot like the Halloween version of Santa). Linus asserts that Santa is only better known because he "gets more publicity." In one of several quietly hilarious scenes, they finally chalk up the root of their disagreement to being "separated by denominational differences."

Charlie Brown gets an invitation to Violet's Halloween party, an infatuated Sally follows Linus to the pumpkin patch, and the rest of the gang goes trick-or-treating. In the meantime, Snoopy dresses up as a World War I flying ace (and imagines dogfighting with the Red Baron over the skies of France), and the trick-or-treaters finally meet up at Violet's holiday bash.

Decks used: *Halloween Tarot, Quest Tarot,* and two cards from the *Universal Waite Tarot*

**The Hierophant:** In some decks, including the *Quest Tarot,* the Hierophant is either renamed Tradition or associated with this particular keyword. I chose this card to represent the forty-plus years of amusement that *It's the Great Pumpkin, Charlie Brown!* has provided to millions of children and kids at heart via its annual TV appearance. I also chose this card because Charlie Brown was always concerned with a sense of morality, of right and wrong. It's the dictates of the Hierophant that often provide a moral compass to many, in the form of parental instruction, religious doctrine, or cultural mores.

**Ace of Pumpkins:** The very beginning of this episode begins with Lucy and Linus picking out a pumpkin from the patch. In the *Halloween Tarot,* the Ace of Pumpkins (correlated with the Ace of Pentacles/Coins) is a smiling jack-o-lantern bucket brimming with assorted candies. This card perfectly captures the festive scene, including the colorful autumn leaves blanketing the ground.

**Knight of Ghosts:** This whimsical knight (the equivalent of the Knight of Cups) delivers a scroll, while a cheery floating ghost gestures as if to say, "For me?" I chose this card to represent the good news Charlie Brown received in the mail: an invitation to Violet's Halloween party.

**Six of Pumpkins:** Two costumed children proffer their bags to a benevolent witch dispensing candy—a perfect image representing the trick-or-treating kids in the TV show. Even in many traditional images of the Six of Pentacles/Coins, the exchange of goods—giving and/or receiving—would be quite fitting for this holiday custom.

**Seven of Stones, Five of Pentacles,** and **Nine of Wands:** I've chosen three cards to represent the complexities of Charlie Brown's character. Charlie never seems to get the girl, get the grades, or get the winning catch. He's a failure in his own eyes and everyone else's. In fact, when Charlie receives the invitation to Violet's party, Lucy nastily observes that it had to be a mistake.

Charlie intends to be a ghost for Halloween, but because he got carried away cutting out eyeholes with the scissors, his white sheet ends up full of holes. While trick-or-treating, the rest of the kids report on their booty after each house (a chocolate bar! a popcorn ball!), but Charlie Brown receives the same thing every time: a rock. How appropriate that the Seven of Stones from the *Quest Tarot* shows seven gray rocks suspended in midair, looking just like the ones tossed in Charlie Brown's bag. And how appropriate that the keyword the *Quest Tarot* assigns to this card is "failure."

One of the aspects I see in the Universal Waite's Five of Pentacles card is the quintessential outsider, either real or imagined. According to the PBS documentary *American Masters: Good Ol' Charles Schulz*, the *Peanuts* creator often felt as though he were an outsider, projecting this feeling, and that of not being good enough, onto his main character. In *It's the Great Pumpkin, Charlie Brown!*, a girl approaches Charlie Brown at the party, exclaiming that he's the "perfect model." Thrilled at this compliment, he readily accompanies the girl to a table. His excitement soon turns to disappointment and humiliation, however, when she turns him around and uses the back of his bald head as the canvas for the sketch of a jack-o-lantern face.

Yet despite all the rejection, Charlie Brown never gives up. Like the battered and bruised man in the Universal Waite Nine of Wands, Charlie perseveres (and continues to trust) despite remembering all the times when he was the butt of jokes or the odd man out. Somehow, Charlie continually picks himself up after each stumble, prank, or embarrassment.

**Nine of Swords:** Those familiar with the Peanuts cartoon strip and the various animated specials will remember that a running gag depicts

Lucy holding a football and encouraging Charlie Brown to kick it, only to pull it away at the last minute, time and time again. When I think of Lucy, the first card that comes to mind is the Nine of Swords (keyword: "cruelty") from the *Quest Tarot*, because of her constant betrayal of Charlie Brown's trust (admittedly arising out of his own inability to learn from the past), as well as her acid tongue and condescension. In the companion book to the *Quest Tarot*, author Joseph Ernest Martin writes this about the Nine of Swords: "People act with the intent to hurt you deeply. Feeling cut apart and broken by circumstances beyond your control . . . Someone stands ready to stab a knife into your back. Betrayal."

**Ace of Cups:** At the Halloween party, Schroeder plays a series of piano pieces. He segues from happy to morose tunes, and Snoopy reacts accordingly. For the lively melodies, Snoopy reacts exuberantly, but when the tune turns gloomy, the expressive beagle begins to sob. The *Quest Tarot*'s keyword for this particular card is "emotion," so I chose the card to represent the fullness and range of emotion that Snoopy readily displays in response to Schroeder's impassioned performance.

**Page of Imps** and **the Hanged Man:** In the *Halloween Tarot*, the Page of Imps (equivalent to other decks' Page of Wands) carries a flaming torch, an apt symbol for Linus and his unabashed zeal for the Great Pumpkin, as well as his sense of adventure, individuality, and optimism that this being will appear as expected, bearing bagfuls of candy.

Although Sally reminds Linus that he'll miss all the Halloween merriment if he stays up for the Great Pumpkin, he willingly sacrifices the sure thing of a party and trick-or-treating for something greater. I can't help but think of the Universal Waite's Hanged Man as a Christ figure who sacrifices the sure bet of popularity, accolades, and possible gain for a higher calling that has a much richer reward in his eyes. Linus waits for the Great Pumpkin, although he has his own Gethsemane experience when he questions the legitimacy of his decision.

**Two of Bats:** In his moment of doubt in the pumpkin patch, Linus remarks to the yet-to-arrive Great Pumpkin, "If you really are a fake, don't tell me. I don't want to know." The costumed angel in this Halloween Tarot card wears a blindfold, and her arms are crossed in front of her chest. I tend to see this as a "look the other way" or "refusing to see" card—a person who chooses to disregard what is in front of her rather than face up to a harsh reality. Or, remembering the red pill versus blue pill debate in the first *Matrix* movie, I tend to see this as the "blue pill" card—where a person would rather live in a comfortable illusion than an uneasy existence of the truth.

**Four of Cups:** The keywords for this Quest Tarot card are "mixed emotions," and that's exactly what Linus exhibits, especially toward the end of the night. On one hand, he wants to follow the path of the faithful, but in the face of a doubting (and eventually irate) Sally, he wavers for a moment. When he catches himself saying "*if* he [the Great Pumpkin] comes," Linus gasps in horror, noting that he's "doomed" because such a slip could cost him the favor of the Great Pumpkin, who honors only sincerity, not hypocrisy.

**Eight of Swords:** When the Great Pumpkin doesn't show, Sally is livid. She regrets staying in the pumpkin patch with Linus, bemoaning the fact that she missed trick-or-treating for nothing. She calls Linus a blockhead, blames him for ruining her night, exclaims that she's going to sue, and demands restitution. In the *Universal Waite*, the Eight of Swords shows a woman who appears loosely bound by strips of cloth. I tend to associate this card with those who are "sue happy," as well as those who blame others for the results of their own choices and then play the whiny victim. The *Quest Tarot* gives this card the keyword "interference," and Sally certainly feels that Linus interfered with her Halloween festivities, although it was her choice to go with him (or not).

**The Star:** The next day, Linus shares his disappointment with Charlie Brown. Next thing we know, eager anticipation bubbles up, and Linus exclaims that he's certain the Great Pumpkin will show up next year. The keyword for the Star in the *Quest Tarot* is "hope." For Linus, hope springs eternal, year after delightful year.

## COMMENTARY

Although some link the Six of Cups with nostalgia and fond childhood memories, my gut instinct was to pick the Hierophant instead to represent *It's the Great Pumpkin, Charlie Brown!* Watching this annual TV special not only has been a tradition of mine for years, but it's also one I am passing on to my son. Lucy Cavendish renames the Hierophant card Tradition in her *Oracle Tarot* deck, just as the *Quest Tarot* does, and connects it with nostalgia.

In Tarot decks such as the *Quest Tarot*, *Thoth Tarot*, and *Oracle Tarot*, keywords are printed right on the card. Some Tarot enthusiasts spurn such decks because keywords are either too distracting or purport to tell the reader what a card *should* mean. For those new to Tarot, however, decks with keywords can offer welcome assistance for interpretations. In addition, a deck creator's unique set of keywords or phrases can supply fresh perspectives on a card or cards.

Some deck creators rename not only Major Arcana cards, but also Minor Arcana suits. In the *Halloween Tarot*, the fire/wands suit becomes the suit of imps, the earth/pentacles suit becomes the suit of pumpkins, the air/swords becomes the suit of bats, and the water/cups suit is renamed the suit of ghosts. In the *Quest Tarot*, the earth/pentacles suit becomes the suit of stones.

Other creators add one or several additional cards to the traditional seventy-eight. For example, with a nod to quantum physics and the idea of parallel universes, Joseph Ernest Martin adds an additional card to the *Quest Tarot's* Major Arcana: the Multiverse (keyword: "unbound"). He assigns the number zero to this card, the same designation assigned to the Fool of the *Quest Tarot* and many other decks.

## YOUR TURN

— What were your favorite comic strips, cartoons, or children's shows as a youth, or perhaps even now? Why did they appeal to you? Choose cards that remind you of the characters, story lines, and associated memories.

— Have you ever witnessed an incident in which someone acted like a bully or gave out unsolicited advice (or criticism) to anyone within earshot? What cards seem to symbolize the people involved, as well as the interactions and the outcome?

— Think of a famous individual who persevered despite great odds. Alternatively, consider a movie or book character that exemplified the underdog archetype. Which cards would you select to represent the circumstances, as well as the character and tenacity of the person?

# THE WIZARD OF OZ

*Janet Boyer*

Released in 1939 to high acclaim, *The Wizard of Oz* remains one of the most-watched movies in cinematic history. Based on the 1900 novel *The Wonderful Wizard of Oz* by L. Frank Baum, this enchanted tale, featuring singing munchkins, apple-throwing trees, and flying monkeys, continues to delight audiences worldwide. Dorothy Gale, the Scarecrow, the Tin Man, and the Cowardly Lion make for a whimsical cast of characters, while the winding yellow brick road, vast field of red poppies, and sparkling Emerald City stimulate the imaginations of both young and old.

Decks used: *Universal Waite Tarot* and one card from the *Tarot of Oz*

**Four of Cups:** At the beginning of the movie, a restless Dorothy tries to get the ranch hands to play with her, only to interfere with their work and incur the anger of her Auntie Em. Feeling bored with her life, she fails to see the good around her—much like the figure in the Universal Waite Four of Cups, who sits with arms crossed, focusing on the three empty cups on the ground. The fourth cup, offered by a hand emerging from a cloud, goes unnoticed.

**Two of Wands:** Dorothy begins to sing "Over the Rainbow," pining for a trouble-free life amid clear skies, flying bluebirds, and dreams that come true. When I see the man in the Universal Waite Two of Wands pondering a globe in his hand, open vistas before him, I'm reminded of Dorothy wanting to forsake her ordinary life for a new world of adventure.

**Queen of Swords:** Toto trespasses into the yard of nasty spinster Miss Gulch one too many times, and she arrives at the Gale farm with the law in tow. Brandishing a paper from the sheriff, she orders Aunt Em and Uncle Henry to place Toto in a basket so she can take the dog away. At her worst, I see the Queen of Swords in most decks as a critical woman with too much time on her hands, perhaps trying to assuage her own loneliness and disappointment by meddling in the affairs of others, even to the point of attempting to get others in trouble or using the law to enforce her expectations or ideas of right and wrong.

**The Tower:** Dorothy sets out to find Toto and comes across a traveling magician known as Professor Marvel. This kindly charlatan pretends to read Dorothy's mind and tries to scare her into going home by "foretelling" that Auntie Em is sick. On the way back, a tornado kicks up, and Dorothy gets a smack on the head—literally. I tend to see the Tower as symbolizing unexpected and stressful circumstances that force us to deconstruct the familiar. Like such circumstances, Professor Marvel and the Wizard both serve as catalysts for Dorothy's "aha" moments.

**The Hanged Man:** When actress Judy Garland uttered the phrase "Toto, I've a feeling we're not in Kansas anymore," she probably had no inkling that this sentence would work its way into pop culture as shorthand for out-of-the-ordinary situations. There are times that we encounter a "reality" that seems so far-fetched or bizarre that we feel disoriented. Special effects and evocative storytelling can produce this feeling, as can music, sculpture, and theater.

As Dorothy enters some kind of dream state after her whack on the head, the familiar suddenly converts into something fantastical—especially as Miss Gulch transforms into a broom-riding witch.

This alternate reality is the realm of the Hanged Man, where right side up appears to invert before our very eyes. In *The Wizard of Oz*, the opening scenes are in black and white, but when Dorothy opens her bedroom door, a burst of polychromatic splendor signifies her entrance into a magical world. In my opinion, this brilliant visual is one of the best illustrations of the sudden before-and-after feeling that comes with entering such wildly altered circumstances—the same feeling the Universal Waite card evokes.

**The Devil:** Both the Wicked Witch of the East (the one originally wearing the ruby slippers and killed by the house) and the Wicked Witch of the West engendered fear. All through the movie, the sister of the dead witch pursues Dorothy and her friends, spying on them via her crystal ball, interfering with their progress, and throwing obstacles in their way. The Devil card in the *Universal Waite* shows two figures chained to the very block the devil sits upon—an apt visual metaphor for the inability to escape from loathsome people or circumstances.

**Six of Wands:** At first, Dorothy feels bad that she killed someone, especially as word spreads throughout Munchkin Land, but she receives a boisterous reception as a liberator and victor. The Universal Waite Six of Wands shows a man riding on a horse amid a crowd, with what appears to be laurel wreaths of accomplishment sitting atop his head and staff.

**The High Priestess:** I see Glinda, the Good Witch of the North, as the High Priestess in that she knows much but says little, choosing to give Dorothy rather vague instructions on how to get back home. Although Glinda knows from the outset that clicking the heels of the ruby slippers will send Dorothy home, she never tells her. When the Scarecrow confronts Glinda toward the end of the movie, asking why she didn't tell Dorothy earlier, Glinda responds, "She wouldn't have believed me. She had to learn it for herself."

The lessons of the High Priestess are not obvious or didactic like those of the Hierophant or perhaps even the Hermit. No, the wisdom she imparts lies in a mirror; each individual must look within to access the way back "home." As Dorothy notes, "If I ever go looking for my heart's desire again, I won't look any further than my own backyard. Because if it isn't there, I never really lost it to begin with!"

**Page of Swords:** Although Toto never talks, he is spunky and fearless, often helping Dorothy find her way through treacherous circumstances along the yellow brick road. The youthful impudence of a page combined with the clarity of the swords suit make this particular card seem quite apt for brave Toto (especially when he's the one to reveal the "man behind the curtain").

**The Fool:** Arguably the best card in the deck to indicate frolicsome abandon and pratfalls, I chose the Fool to represent the lovable, brainless Scarecrow.

**Strength:** Facing our fears with courage, feeling afraid but doing it anyway—the Cowardly Lion exemplifies these phrases perfectly, so it's no surprise that some Tarotists consider this the "Cowardly Lion" card.

**Ace of Cups:** In the *Tarot of Oz* deck by David Sexton, the central image of the Ace of Cups is the head of the Tin Man. This image seems an appropriate designation for the Ace of Cups, especially since the Tin Man longed to have a heart. In fact, the Minor Arcana of the Tarot mirrors the four suits of traditional playing cards: diamonds correspond to pentacles, spades correlate to swords, clubs correspond to wands, and hearts become cups. The Ace of Cups would be the same as the Ace of Hearts—a fitting symbol for the Tin Woodsman who thought he didn't have one.

**The Magician:** Actor Frank Morgan played four parts in the movie: Professor Marvel, the gatekeeper of Oz, the coach driver of the horse of many colors, and the "powerful" Wizard of Oz.

On one hand, Professor Marvel is a con man and the wizard an imposter. But when Dorothy calls him a bad man, he protests that he's actually a good man, just a very poor wizard. When the Tin Man and Cowardly Lion ask about the Scarecrow's brain, he replies, "Why, anybody can have a brain. That's a very mediocre commodity! Every pusillanimous creature that crawls on the earth or slinks through slimy seas has a brain!"

Ah, the man behind the curtain is quite eloquent! Mercury (both the planet and the god) is often associated with the Magician card. In mythology, it was said that Mercury was born with a silver tongue that could influence and persuade. (And, of course, liquid Mercury is known as "quicksilver.") Most charlatans are smooth talkers, but it would appear that this particular trickster has more wisdom than first appears.

In the book *What Story Are You Living?* by Carol Pearson and Hugh Marr, the authors observe, "Changing the world by an alteration in perception and in language is the power of the archetype called the Magician." The wizard does not give the Scarecrow a "real" brain, or the Tin Man a "real" heart, or the Lion "real" courage. However, when they receive a diploma, a ticking heart, and a shiny medal, respectively, the travelers appear to transform before our very eyes. This Magician has deftly shifted their perception of themselves by the act of changing ordinary objects into talismans of empowerment.

**Ten of Cups:** There are many memorable quotes from *The Wizard of Oz*, but "There's no place like home" has to be one of the most widely used today. When Dorothy wakes up in her bedroom, surrounded by her friends and family (and even a concerned Professor Marvel), she is thankful for the love and care that have always encircled her. When I think of the Ten of Cups, I think of the warmth of a loving family and faithful friends that often surround us but are all too often taken for granted in these busy times.

## COMMENTARY

The *Tarot of Oz* by David Sexton is a unique deck based on the entire Baum series, which spans fifteen books. Interestingly, Sexton chooses the cyclone to represent his Wheel of Fortune card. Although something like a storm or change of fortune would certainly make sense for the Wheel card, I feel that Dorothy's profound insight that she already had what she most wanted is more indicative of the Tower card, in which illumination of the lighting strike means our tower will never be quite the same again. Early in the movie, we get a foreshadowing of her tower of apathy cracking after she sees Professor Marvel, because she laments to Toto that "Auntie Em was so good to me. And I never appreciated it. Running away and hurting her feelings. . . ."

After I wrote the section on the High Priestess, I remembered that the *Lo Scarabeo Tarot* actually shows its version of the High Priestess gazing into what looks to be a handheld mirror, which speaks to me of someone looking within for answers.

## Your Turn

— Chances are you're quite familiar with *The Wizard of Oz* film, or even the Baum book series. Recall when you first encountered Dorothy and company. With which character did you most identify? What about now? If you were to change anything about the story or movie, what would it be and why? Create a BIT Snapshot by choosing the cards you feel represent these components of your Oz memories.

— Think of a time when someone you knew didn't get what they wished for but got exactly what they needed. How were their life and perspective expanded? What cards seem to capture this scenario?

— Having a main character endure a rite of passage, meet a test of strength, or overcome a seemingly insurmountable obstacle is a common motif in books and film. In *The Wizard of Oz*, the wizard charges Dorothy with the task of retrieving the witch's broom as a condition of granting their requests. Recall a movie or story in which the main character goes on a quest. What is the goal? Did they get what they were after or did they discover something better (or worse)? Select cards that represent what happened.

# How the Grinch Stole Christmas
### *Janet Boyer*

Widely known by his pen name Dr. Seuss, author Theodor Geisel (1904–1991) created a cast of lovable characters and wacky worlds in his children's books. From Horton to the Lorax, the Cat in the Hat to Marvin K. Mooney, Dr. Seuss's whimsical characters entertain children through dozens of books, some of which have been turned into animated specials and feature films.

One of the most famous of Seuss's characters is the leering green meanie with "termites in his smile" and "garlic in his soul": the despicable Mr. Grinch. Based on the children's book, the TV classic *How the Grinch Stole Christmas* features the voice talent of Boris Karloff (who played Frankenstein's Monster and starred in other horror films), animation by Chuck Jones (who also drew the Warner Bros.' characters the Road Runner, Bugs Bunny, and Pepe Le Pew), and special song lyrics by Seuss himself. This amusing tale of redemption takes viewers from the Grinch's mountainous cave down to the cheery hamlet of Whoville, where the "cuddly as a cactus" villain attempts to wipe out Christmas.

Deck used: *Universal Waite Tarot*

**Ten of Cups:** The story begins with a circle of joyous creatures called Whos singing in the center of Whoville. Besides thinking of a happy family when I see the Ten of Cups, I also associate this card with harmonious relationships and cooperation. Some renderings of the Ten of Cups show children holding hands or couples embracing—fitting images for the good-natured Whos!

**Four of Wands** and **Seven of Cups:** Given the Whos' dizzying array of musical contraptions, festive boisterousness, and glorious feasting, the celebratory Four of Wands just didn't seem to be enough to capture the wonder of the Whos. Although the Seven of Cups can be a "castles in the air" card, I tend to view this card with great fondness: so many choices, so many opportunities—which do I focus on today? I sometimes think of the Seven of Cups as the "life is a buffet" card. The Whos seem to have many material distractions readily available, and they enjoy them immensely. As the end of this story shows, however, their contentment arises from something much deeper and is independent of frills, thrills, and even food.

**Five of Swords** and **Seven of Swords:** For more than fifty years, the Grinch put up with the happy Whos. One day, a menacing smirk creeps upon his visage when he gets a "wonderful, awful idea": "What a great Grinchy trick! With this coat and hat, I'll look just like Saint Nick!" I chose the Five of Swords to express this sentiment because the Universal Waite version depicts what appears to be a gloating man, as well as two other figures who are walking away, perhaps dejectedly. Because the Grinch has a heart "two sizes too small," the jubilation of the Whos sets his teeth on edge, and he's determined to destroy what he thinks is the source of their happiness. The Grinch feels that it's him against them, and he plots to ruin the Whos' Christmas by demoralizing them, assuming they'll cry "boo hoo" when they discover that everything—light bulbs, poinsettia petals, and even ice cubes—has been taken from them.

The Seven of Swords shows a figure walking away from a group of tents with an armload of blades—a picture that some interpret as theft. When the Grinch stealthily takes every bauble, morsel, and stocking from Whoville, he resembles the figure on the Seven of Swords.

I also tend to think of the Seven of Swords as the "wolf in sheep's clothing" card in certain instances. When little Cindy Lou Who catches the Grinch taking away their decorations, the "smart and slick" Grinch, dressed in a Santa suit, thinks up a lie on the spot: he quickly notices a burned-out light on the Christmas tree and tells her that he's taking the entire tree to his workshop to fix it. The Grinch goes so far as to give Cindy Lou a drink, patting her on the head with faux kindness.

**Six of Cups:** With her wide-eyed innocence, Cindy Lou Who embodies the naivete of children. In her world, it's inconceivable that someone would brashly enter her house and steal everything for the express purpose of causing grief. She believes that the Grinch is indeed Santa, and her trust borders on heartbreaking. Originally, I thought of the Sun card to represent Cindy Lou Who, but this scenario reminded me of the times when a trusting child is left in the presence of a predatory adult, and the pain and loss that can often ensue. (If you look closely at the Universal Waite image, a guard seems to be ascending the stairs to the left, leaving the child unattended in the presence of a looming figure.)

In the *Universal Waite Tarot*, the Six of Cups shows this taller figure handing a cup of flowers to a little girl. This person appears to be wearing an elflike costume and is almost double the size of the little girl. Although this card is sometimes interpreted as reconciliation, nostalgia, innocence, sharing, compassion, simple gifts, and childhood, there seems to be a sinister element to the Rider-Waite rendering of the Six of Cups when viewed in a particular light. I felt this was an apt choice to represent the scene in which Cindy Lou gently confronts "Santa."

**The Devil:** The Grinch enslaves his dog, Max, forcing him to carry loads much heavier than his little body. A circular attachment connects the dog's harness to the Grinch's getaway sleigh. Interestingly, in the Universal Waite image, a similar circular fixture connects the Devil's perch to the enchained humans.

The Grinch wrongly assumes that depriving the Whos of their material goods will result in sadness and despair. The flip side to this belief is, of course, that material abundance brings joy and contentment. To me, one of the representations of the Devil card is the insatiable belief that things equal happiness or that the relentless pursuit of the new and improved will fill an emotional void. Because the Grinch thinks that materialism is the source of the Whos' well-being, he assumes taking just about everything they own is the same as stealing Christmas from them.

**Judgement:** On Christmas morning, the Grinch gleefully anticipates the wailing of the Whos, but boy is he in for a surprise! Instead of hearing boo hoos, a "glad sound reached his ears. All the Whos were singing without any toys. Somehow or another, Christmas came anyway! It came without ribbons, tags, packages, or bags!" It is in that moment that the Grinch has an epiphany: "Maybe Christmas . . . doesn't come from a store—maybe it means a little bit more."

When the Grinch sees the error of his ways, he has a literal "change of heart," because his heart "grew three sizes that day." He blew on his trumpet, returned all the games, food, and decorations, and even joined the Whos at the supper table, carving the roast beast. When I see the trumpet-blowing angel in the Judgement card from the *Universal Waite*, I think of a wake-up call that results in changed behavior—just like the Grinch experienced.

**Ten of Cups:** I chose this card to frame the beginning *and* the end of *How the Grinch Stole Christmas* because the Whos' joy and well-being remained the same, independent of the machinations of the Grinch and their personal losses. The end of this heartwarming story sums up my view of the Ten of Cups quite nicely: "Christmas day will always be just as long as we have we. Welcome Christmas while we stand, heart to heart and hand in hand."

## COMMENTARY

One of the ways I see the Judgement card is "turning over a new leaf," or the realization that some approach or belief system just isn't working. Whether this conscious acknowledgment comes as a result of the Tower, the Devil, the Hanged Man, or other archetypal energy, the "aha" moment of realizing what will invite or promote our personal heaven on earth can be a gloriously pivotal moment. (Two great books on this topic are *Loving What Is* by Byron Katie and *What God Wants* by Neale Donald Walsch).

## Your Turn

— Think of a time when you assumed you needed something specific to make you happy. Did obtaining that item, relationship, or experience turn out to make you happy over the long haul? How has your idea of what supports well-being and joy changed over the years? Choose corresponding cards to map your progress and present attitudes toward happiness.

— Have you ever witnessed a situation in which an individual assumed that in order to alleviate their own sense of lack or low self-esteem, they had to steal, bully, or otherwise prove themselves? What cards would you select to represent the circumstances and people involved?

— Can you think of an event from history, a recent news story, a book, or a movie in which a devastating loss occurred, but the individuals involved retained good humor and buoyancy despite their circumstances? What cards seem to symbolize the event and subsequent reactions?

# Headlines and History

## PARIS HILTON, JAILBIRD
### *Janet Boyer*

**B**orn into a wealthy family that made its fortune with a worldwide hotel chain, heiress Paris Hilton has often been derided as "being famous for being famous." Some have argued, however, that she has worked for her fame by selling her own fragrances and jewelry line, appearing on a reality TV show, and taking acting gigs. A noted partier, Paris was busted for driving under the influence (DUI) several times. After driving without a license, she was sentenced to jail in 2007, eventually serving twenty-two days in a Los Angeles County prison.

Deck used: *Universal Waite Tarot*

**The Star:** From all the coverage Paris received from tabloids, TV news channels, and entertainment magazines, she is obviously a "star." Considering that the female figure in the Star card is nude, I can't help but remember Paris's infamous sex video that made its rounds on the Internet.

**Page of Cups:** The Page of Cups shows a youth gazing into a cup that holds a fish. I sometimes see this card as indicating escapism, shallowness, and even sexual promiscuity. It seemed appropriate to couple this card with the dumb-blonde persona. I chose this card because pages can often represent children. Because of the connection of the cups suit to emotions,

I felt that the Page of Cups represented both her supposed facade of emotional immaturity, as well as her self-absorption.

**Three of Cups:** This card shows three girls partying. Need I say more?

**King of Pentacles:** The original source of the Hilton fortune is Paris's grandfather. As I mentioned previously, I view the King of Pentacles as the "Donald Trump card," indicating someone who handles great amounts of wealth or land—for example, a banker, real estate investor, or syndicate. In her book *Learning the Tarot*, Joan Bunning says that this card "might as well be called King Midas as he turns everything he touches to gold (riches of all kinds)."

**Ten of Pentacles:** I see this as an old-money card. Paris's parents certainly didn't make the Hilton fortune, and the older man in the Universal Waite version of this card reminds me of Paris's grandfather. In this case, I also see this card as an "enabling" card. Blood is thicker than water, so the saying goes, and family members tend to demonize anyone who dares attack one of their own.

**Eight of Swords:** Swords surround the woman in this card, reminding me of a jail cell. During her incarceration, it was reported that Paris suffered from claustrophobia. This card shows a woman bound by strips of cloth and a blindfold, which would no doubt give a claustrophobic the heebie-jeebies.

**The Moon:** There was some secrecy surrounding Hilton's incarceration, including a mystery illness that resulted in her temporary release to house arrest. (It turned out to be attention deficit/hyperactivity disorder [ADHD], although some in the media were speculating about sexually transmitted diseases.) Determining "reality" in the shifting shadows of the moon can be difficult, much like the media grasping for certainty for not only the mystery illness, but also whether Paris was truly remorseful and sincere in her supposed reformation.

**Justice:** Justice obviously deals with court cases and the law, but I chose this card for a different reason. While Paris (and her mom) initially whined about the "unfair" jail sentence, the heiress eventually bucked up and served her time. I assume that her publicist urged her to do her time without complaint to salvage (or remake) her image, convince the public that justice was served, and to demonstrate that a contrite Paris didn't think she was above the law of the land.

**The High Priestess:** After Paris was released from jail, she was seen with several self-help books (including Eckhart Tolle's *The Power of Now*). Some felt it was a public-relations stunt to depict her as a serious, studious person concerned with spiritual matters. She admitted to interviewers that she had never been alone before her incarceration and wanted to "know herself." The High Priestess card is a fitting choice because the woman on the card holds a scroll of sacred knowledge, which can represent intuition and trusting one's own inner guidance.

**Seven of Swords:** I chose this card to represent Paris's first post-jail interview with CNN's Larry King. Though tempted to pick a king card because of the name, I chose the Seven of Swords. I see this card as indicating diplomacy, strategy, and cunning. When asked how he gets his guests to reveal so much, King once said that he never approaches a guest with accusations or belligerence, choosing to ask open-ended questions in a nonthreatening manner. The questions he asks are those to which he thinks his audience wants answers. By taking this avuncular approach, famous people often share revealing anecdotes and information during his interviews.

**Eight of Wands:** In the interview with Larry King, Paris revealed that she received an avalanche of supportive letters from the public (including soldiers overseas). When I see the Eight of Wands, I often think of rapid or voluminous communication, including e-mails, telephone messages, and snail-mail letters.

**Six of Pentacles:** Post-incarceration, Paris said she wanted to focus on philanthropy. For many months, she stayed out of the headlines except for reports on her charity work. I chose the Six of Pentacles for her intended direction since the man in this card carries a scale while dispensing coins to kneeling beggars.

Speaking of philanthropy, Paris's grandfather donated most of his fortune to charity within a year of her incarceration, cutting her future inheritance from an estimated $100 million to about $5 million. I have to wonder if Paris had kept her nose clean (and clothes on) all these years, would her granddaddy have proceeded with his hefty bequest?

## COMMENTARY

Whereas the High Priestess often indicates inner wisdom and even esotericism, the Hierophant represents, to me, exoteric spirituality as embodied by formal religion and members of the clergy. In addition, I see the Hierophant as legislating and enforcing morality (or at least trying to), whereas the High Priestess follows a higher law born of the Spirit. If the Hierophant is the letter of the law, then the High Priestess is the spirit of the law.

In many decks, the Three of Cups shows three women holding aloft cups in obvious celebration. Although I picked this card to represent Paris's clubbing and partying with her gal pals, I also see this card as the "coffee klatch" card, as well as representing gab sessions, gossip, and cliques.

## YOUR TURN

— Can you think of a time when you acted contrary to someone's idea of right or wrong, or perhaps even broke the law? Did you get away with anything, or did you have to pay for your actions? Select cards to represent the people, actions, feelings, thoughts, and results that occurred.

- Do you know of someone who was the object of gossip or disrepute? Were the allegations slanderous or true to life? Did the person ever change as the result of their notoriety, or did they stay true to their path? Which cards remind you of the people and rumors involved?

- Can you think of a notorious figure who served jail time in the media spotlight? What about a renowned prisoner of war or human-rights activist incarcerated for their political or spiritual beliefs? Choose cards to represent the prisoner, law enforcement officers, legal or political analysts, ideology, antagonists, sympathizers, or anyone else involved in the situation.

## ALEXANDER GRAHAM BELL: INVENTOR EXTRAORDINAIRE

*Janet Boyer*

Born in Scotland on March 3, 1847, to a father who was a speech teacher and a mother who was an accomplished deaf pianist, Alexander Graham Bell assumed he'd grow up to be a musician, especially since he could play a song on the piano after hearing it but once. Homeschooled and always curious, young Alec, as his parents called him, began inventing at a young age. His first invention was born of a reprimand given by his friend's father. After fooling around near a flour mill, Mr. Herdman admonished Alec and his friend to "do something useful," such as find a way to remove the husks of grain from wheat. After rooting around in the barn for parts, Alec did just that, making the husker his first invention.

Alec eventually moved to Canada with his parents in 1870, and in 1871, he began teaching deaf children in Boston. Fascinated by the telegraph, Alex was convinced he could send multiple sounds, even human voices, over electrical wires. The father of one of his deaf students, Gardiner Hubbard, was impressed with Alec's ideas and funded his exploits. Alec collaborated with Thomas Watson, whom he met at an electricity workshop, largely because Watson was good with his hands. About the same time, Alec fell in love with and fervently pursued one of his students. After a few years, his kindness won over Mabel Hubbard, and they were married on July 11, 1877.

Mabel's father eventually convinced Alec to file for a patent application for the telephone. It's a good thing that Mr. Hubbard urged Alec to do so, because Graham Bell had to defend his patent in court more than six hundred times, including against Thomas Edison and the Western Union Company. Although Alexander Graham Bell is most famous for the telephone, he also invented a metal detector (used in several wars to find bullets in wounded men) and a metal jacket to aid breathing. He also went on to set a world speed record with his hydrofoil (a type of boat). Alec eventually began to write for the National Geographic Society, which was started by his father-in-law. Under his direction as president, *National Geographic* magazine flourished, guided by Alec's slogan, "The world and all that's in it."

Deck used: *Universal Waite Tarot*

**King of Wands** and **Eight of Pentacles:** I chose these two cards to represent Alexander Graham Bell (just one wouldn't do!). Always on the lookout for new projects into which to channel his passionate creativity, Alec took risks, attracted imitators, and generated "buzz." His pioneering ideas and solutions never stayed in the realm of ideas, however, as perhaps the Knight of Wands and his trail of unfinished projects might indicate, which is why I selected the King of Wands to represent the curiosity and fervor that fueled his inventions. Alec always put feet under his theories, often working long hours to the point of forgetting to eat. This absorption in his work likely ran his body ragged, which could have contributed to the diabetic complications that led to his death in 1922. Just like the man in the Eight of Pentacles hammering away on a pentacle at his workbench, Alec pursued his ideas with an almost unhealthy dedication.

**The Magician:** Traditionally, this card is associated with the god Mercury, or Hermes. Because many of Alec's inventions involved communication—including creating "visible speech" with his father and brothers—this messenger god, as represented by the Magician, seems an apt symbol of Bell's most significant achievements.

**Justice:** Because this card often deals with legalities, I chose Justice to represent the filing of Graham Bell's telephone patent, as well as the hundreds of successful cases defending it. Although he hated being involved in lawsuits, he realized that he stood to lose great sums of money if others were to usurp his patented processes.

**The Hierophant:** Alec began as a teacher, and I associate the Hierophant with formal education, so it seemed fitting to pair the educational aspects of this card with Alec's passion for helping deaf students. His father helped students overcome stuttering, so it would seem that Alec followed his father's example in this regard.

**Knight of Cups:** Mabel was seventeen when Alec fell in love with her (he was twenty-eight at the time). Although she respected her teacher, she didn't think she could return his feelings at first. I chose the Knight of Cups, the "hopeless romantic" card, to represent Alec's pursuit of Mabel, whose heart he eventually won.

**The Lovers:** I tend to think of the Two of Cups as the soul-mate card, but I chose the Lovers to represent not only Alec and Mabel's marriage, but also the true partnership that they seemed to have. She supported Alec's work, including his long hours in the lab, especially by looking after his physical well-being, which he often neglected when left to his own devices.

**Queen of Pentacles:** Mabel not only took care of Bell's physical needs, but also administered all their finances. She was an able manager of all things material, allowing Bell the freedom to pursue his work with the deaf and his multiple inventions.

**The Fool:** Some time ago, I saw a biography of Bell on TV in which his great-grandson relayed a story about the famed inventor: Once, when Bell was amidst a small group of men, a child walked up and asked him a question. The other men tried to shoo the child away, but Bell told them to welcome a child's questions and ideas because children have the ability to see with an uncluttered mind. One of the ways I see the energy of the Fool card is as a state of not knowing—lacking the entanglement of prejudice, assumption, and belief. It seems to me that Bell's openness, as well as his ability to see beyond the surface, falls under the aegis of the unnumbered trump. In fact, Bell encountered the seemingly hopeless case of an angry girl named Helen Keller, in whom he saw enormous potential. It was Bell who paired Anne Sullivan, the teacher dubbed "the Miracle Worker," with Keller. He became a lifelong friend of the inspirational activist and lecturer.

**Three of Pentacles:** Although Alexander Graham Bell generated brilliant inventions and solutions, he paired up with Thomas Watson because of his friend's dexterity. A hands-on craftsman diligently working under the supervision of his visionary partner reminds me of the Universal Waite's version of the Three of Pentacles. This image shows an apron-clad workman with tools, standing on a bench near an archway, while two figures, one holding what looks to be a blueprint of sorts, consult with the busy workman.

## COMMENTARY

The kings of the Tarot are often considered the masters of their respective fields. Though it could be argued that Alec was an "idea man" and therefore could be associated with the swords/air/mental realm, I chose the King of

Wands for him because he had not only an abundance of brilliant ideas, but also the passionate wherewithal to do something about them, which led him in other directions of discovery and invention. I associate his infectious enthusiasm and ability to inspire with the fiery wands suit rather than the pure (and often dry or even arrogant) ivory-tower intellectualism that can be associated with the swords suit.

When it came to Mabel, however, Alec had an amorous disposition. In astrology, Alec was a dreamy Pisces, the sign that Teresa Michelsen assigns to the Knight of Cups in her book *The Complete Tarot Reader*.

## YOUR TURN

— Think of a time in your life when your interest and enthusiasm soared. What was the object of your attention? Choose cards to represent your passion and the outcome of your focus.

— Recall a situation in which you observed someone obsessed with a person, object, job, or task. What happened? Which cards would you pick to represent the people, actions, and outcome?

— When you think of great inventors and innovators who have influenced humanity or industry, who comes to mind? Select the cards you feel best exemplify the various aspects of that person's impact.

# BTK: THE DEVIL PERSONIFIED
### Janet Boyer

For two decades, a serial killer terrorized the Wichita, Kansas, area. After his brutal killings, he sent letters to police and media outlets, boasting of his crimes and taunting them with his knowledge of details. For many years, this unknown killer was silent. Then, in 2004, his taunts resumed. Known as BTK, which stands for his modus operandi of "bind, torture, kill," Dennis Rader sent a note to police in February 2005, asking if writings contained on a floppy disk were traceable. Replying via a newspaper ad, the police assured him that it was fine to send the disk. Rader's misplaced trust was his undoing, because the floppy disk he finally sent to the police was indeed traceable. The police traced the disk to a Lutheran church where Rader was president of the church council.

Authorities had collected DNA samples from the various murders and, not wanting to tip off BTK who once threatened to blow up his "lair" if cops found him, brainstormed ways to get familial DNA to connect him with the crimes. One of the investigators remembered that Rader's daughter, Kerri, had attended his alma mater, Kansas State University. Knowing that all the students used the school's medical facilities, he visited the university clinic and found out that Kerri had indeed visited it. He then returned the next day with a court order for her medical records.

Several hours after Rader's arrest on a quiet street near his house, authorities informed Rader that they had DNA matches from both saliva and semen found at a crime scene. It was then that Rader confessed to ten murders committed between 1974 and 1991. Four months later, Rader pled guilty to ten counts of first-degree murder and was sentenced to ten life sentences in El Dorado Correctional Facility. Because all the murders occurred before Kansas reinstated the death penalty, BTK avoided lethal injection.

Deck used: *Universal Waite Tarot*

**The Devil** and **the Hierophant:** It seemed natural to pair the Devil with Rader, especially since the devil is evil personified in many religious traditions. Especially fitting is the chained couple in the foreground, tethered to the very pillar that seats the devil. Dennis Rader was seen as a pillar in the community, serving as a Cub Scout leader, a law enforcement officer, a leading member of the local Republican Party, and a church councilman.

I also picked the Hierophant to represent Rader for three reasons—two being rather obvious: for decades, he was an active member of his church; and the floppy disk that incriminated him was created on the church computer. The third reason is the most disturbing of all: he dragged one of his victims to his church, photographing her in various poses for his sick fantasies.

In his book *Tarot: History, Symbolism, and Divination*, author Robert Place notes, "The Devil makes a perverted sign of benediction to mock the Hierophant." Some associate the Hierophant with traditional authority, and since Rader mocked law enforcement for years with his letters and puzzles, this unholy union between the two cards further represents BTK.

**Eight of Wands:** Astrologically speaking, the Eight of Wands is often associated with Mercury in Sagittarius. The planet Mercury is connected to its namesake, the messenger of the gods, and Sagittarius (the Archer) is often represented by an arrow. Because this astrological attribution makes me think of quick messages, I often associate it with e-mail and instant messaging via computer. I chose this card to represent the floppy disk that eventually connected Dennis Rader to BTK.

**Five of Swords:** When I see the smirking figuring holding three swords "behind the back" of two other figures (two additional swords lie on the ground), I think of Rader taunting the police and news agencies. Swords can indicate the intellect, and Rader certainly felt that he was intellectually superior to the detectives. I'm also reminded of childish attitudes and taunts like "I have something that you don't!"—which, in this case, was the crucial evidence tying Rader to the BTK crimes. The implication of cunning and outsmarting people also refers to the cryptic nature of the puzzles, poems, and letters Rader sent to law enforcement and news outlets.

**Nine of Swords:** A figure sits up in bed, head in hands. Often deemed the nightmare card, I chose this card to represent the tension and anxiety felt around the entire Wichita area as a serial killer remained on the loose for decades. My husband pointed out a motif on the card that I didn't notice until *after* I put all the cards in a line: carved into the bed is a standing figure thrusting a sword toward a seated person. Unfortunately, this picture is an apt portrayal of an aggressive, calculating serial killer, using knives to terrorize his victims as well as haunting a community with his deeds.

**Three of Swords:** I chose this card, which often indicates sorrow, to represent the grief of the victims' friends and family members. A bright red heart impaled by three swords, clouds and rain in the background, this image serves as a fitting representation of loss. As I look at the three swords, I can't help but think of Rader's wife and two children (born *after* Rader's initial murders) and how they felt when this father and husband was revealed to be a monster.

**Two of Swords:** I picked this card, with its blindfolded, seated figure, to represent Rader's wife, Paula. Were there signals that she missed—or ignored? Years before his arrest, she discovered a poem written by her husband about one of BTK's victims ("Shirley Locks"). Disturbed, she confronted Rader, who lied about the poem, insisting that it was for a college assignment. Rader is a poor speller, and, oddly enough, his wife once commented to her husband that he "spelled just like BTK"—an unusual tidbit that Rader revealed in court when he matter-of-factly described his crimes in meticulous detail.

In addition, Paula twice found him in the bathroom, clad in women's clothing and hanging from the door—re-creating the erotic thrill he experienced when binding and suffocating his victims. Early in his killing career, Rader had the audacity to call the police when one of his victims remained undiscovered, and his undisguised voice was broadcast on the local TV newscast. Paula and

Dennis were sitting together in their living room when the segment aired. Paula exclaimed, "BTK sounds just like you do!"

While a married, community-involved serial killer is virtually unheard of in criminal profiling (which factored in BTK's ability to elude law enforcement), I can't help but wonder if Paula took a "see no evil" approach to any suspicions. If there was ever any indecision surrounding her thirty-four-year marriage to Rader, it evaporated when he graphically recounted his crimes in the courtroom. A month later, she filed for divorce, which was granted immediately by a district judge because of the special circumstances.

**The Moon:** In the moonlight, shadows materialize and undulate. Because of its half light, you might think you're seeing one thing when it's really quite another. I see this card, which sometimes denotes deception or the unknown, representing co-workers and acquaintances who were completely in the dark about Rader's double life. Speaking of duality, there are two canines in this card: one a domesticated dog, the other a wolf. In his letters, Rader spoke of "Factor X," the incurable, senseless urge that caused him, and other serial killers, to commit unspeakable crimes. Whether he truly had a good or domesticated side is debatable, but of his wild, instinctual side, we are sure. In fact, in a line from his poem "Black Friday," which laments his capture, Rader says, "The dark side of me has been exposed."

**Seven of Swords:** The Seven of Swords shows a figure walking away from a group of tents with five swords in his hand, while two swords stand upright in the ground. As I was creating my BTK BIT Snapshot, I saw this card and thought of "going into the enemy's camp." At the time, BTK was public enemy number one, and, via DNA, Rader's daughter had some of "the enemy" inside her. Symbolically, part of the enemy was snatched when the investigators obtained her DNA from a college Pap smear. This card is also a good match for the clever analysis of investigators, who surmised that getting DNA from one of Rader's relatives could help them link him to certain killings.

**The Fool:** Criminologists and psychologists often theorize that some criminals, deep down, want to be apprehended. Whether this is true in the case of Dennis Rader is questionable, but his sheer stupidity, perhaps fueled by hubris, baffles me. To assume that the police are going to tell you the truth in answer to your question "Will you be able to trace a floppy disk if I send it to you?" seems foolish and naive—a stark contrast to Rader's detailed planning and execution of his crimes. But as he once acknowledged in one of his letters, "There is no help, no cure, except death or being caught and put away." And if the latter, it would only occur by making a stupid mistake, which Rader did on February 16, 2005.

## COMMENTARY

The suit of swords is often connected to mental processes such as analyzing, planning, and assuming, as well as anxiety and grief. I'm not surprised that I reached for swords cards, five in all, to create my BTK Snapshot.

Speaking of the number five, my husband noticed that the figure in the Seven of Swords was carrying five of the seven swords (corresponding with the way Rader's daughter, Kerri, carried his DNA), which is interesting, since I selected the Five of Swords to represent Rader's cunning, gloating, and arrogance. Another five connection is the Hierophant, which is Trump 5 of the Major Arcana.

My husband also pointed out that the Fool, Nine of Swords, Five of Swords, and Three of Swords all had splashes of red in their images, further representing the bloody components of this BIT Snapshot.

Also, I noticed that the devil holds a torch to the "tail" of the chained male figure. "Torch" sounds like the first part of the word "torture"—the T in BTK.

The fact that several of our insights occurred *after* I laid the selected cards in a line to view the overall story shows me the added benefit of laying out selected cards when creating a BIT Snapshot. Lining up the cards this way can lead to unexpected revelations as you look for further connections.

## YOUR TURN

- Have you ever pretended to be someone or projected a different self from the one most people around you are used to? What cards would you select to represent your motives and the result of your pretension?

- Recall a time when someone you knew acted contrary to your assumptions, expectations, or internal picture of who you thought they were. Re-create your experience using the Tarot.

- Can you think of a notorious figure who practiced deception, perhaps deceiving hundreds or thousands of people? What happened? Select cards to represent the major players, the moment the deception was discovered, and the resulting reactions from all involved.

# CRIKEY! STEVE IRWIN, THE CROCODILE HUNTER
### Janet Boyer

Best known as the Crocodile Hunter, Australian conservationist Steve Irwin captivated people around the world with his showmanship and passion for animals. "Isn't she a *beauty?*" he'd exclaim, while observing a crocodile, bearded dragon, or other wildlife. Steve's father, Bob, was a herpetologist while his mom, Lyn, was an animal rehabilitator. They began what would later become Australia Zoo, which they eventually turned over to their son.

When Steve was six, he received a very special birthday present, something he had always wanted: a python. While other children his age were taking care of cats and dogs, Steve was out catching rodents to feed his snake. In June 1992, Steve married Terri Raines, an American girl he had met just a few months before at the zoo. Both reported that it was "love at first sight" for them, and they spent their honeymoon filming their first wildlife documentary. Steve and Terri eventually had two children, Bindi and Bob.

On September 4, 2006, Steve was snorkeling at the Great Barrier Reef while filming a documentary. In a freak accident, a stingray that Steve was observing flexed its spine, plunging a barb through Steve's heart, killing him quickly.

Deck used: *Universal Waite Tarot*

**The Fool:** The Fool immediately comes to mind when I think of Steve Irwin's unbridled curiosity and wonderment. Some would consider Steve's daring deeds foolish. In fact, he received widespread criticism in 2004 when he fed a saltwater crocodile with one hand while holding his one-month-old son in his other. Steve seemed to approach both humans and wildlife without prejudice or cynicism. From all accounts, it would seem he never met a person or animal he didn't like. I tend to see the Fool card as epitomizing a Magical Child archetype, which embodies these traits.

**Strength:** In the Universal Waite version of this card, a woman gently bends toward a lion. This image is a perfect picture of how Steve interacted with wildlife: with gentleness, understanding, respect, patience, and fearlessness.

**The Magician:** Steve's childlike enthusiasm belied his vast knowledge of wildlife as well as his uncanny ability to handle unpredictable situations. In addition to being a great communicator, he was also a mesmerizing entertainer and skilled environmentalist. He wielded the four tools on the Magician's table with aplomb: as a fiery wildlife warrior (wands); a knowledgeable, persuasive communicator (swords); a warm, expressive friend (cups); and a tireless worker on behalf of endangered animals and habitats (pentacles).

**Two of Wands:** Steve was always up for exploring new lands and making the most out of every moment. What many do not know is that, on Queensland's coast, Steve and his father discovered a new species of turtle that is named for Steve: *Elseya irwini*, or "Irwin's turtle." When I see the figure in the Two of Wands standing on a rooftop, gazing at a globe with a vista before him, I think of Steve's insatiable appetite to document strange creatures and visit unusual terrain.

**Ace of Cups:** This card represents the love at first sight that Steve and Terri experienced. It was a new experience, and new attraction, for both of them. While Terri was enamored with Steve's Tarzan-like presentation at Australia Zoo, he thought Terri was a beautiful "Sheila" (a generic Australian term for a girl). In many ways, their attraction was an unexpected gift from the Universe, the gift of love that they felt viscerally and acted upon quickly.

**Death:** I didn't choose this card to represent Steve's death, but rather his premonition that he would die young. His mom, Lyn, died in a car accident in 2000, and Steve felt that he, too, would die in a crash. In fact, he talked about this possibility with Terri many times. Terri herself felt he would likely die young but never from an encounter with wildlife. Rather, she figured he might fall out of a tree or become embroiled in the crossfire of a foreign country's political unrest.

**The Tower:** Steve's death was a shock to the world, and the manner of death was especially shocking to those who knew and loved him. Of all things that Steve could die from, they would never have suspected that it would be from a member of the animal kingdom. Because of his death, the media attention illuminated Steve's conservation efforts, which may have gotten lost in the boisterousness of his persona. Just like the explosive lightning blows off the turret top in the Tower card, this unexpected manner of death sent shock waves through Steve's family, friends, and fans.

**Ten of Swords:** When I think of the stingray's barb going through Steve's heart, I can't help but think of the Ten of Swords card, which shows a prone figure impaled with ten swords in the back. Some believe that it wasn't the barb that killed Steve, but rather the act of pulling the barb out of his chest.

I also chose this card to represent Terri's grief, which was palpable, both at the public memorial service at the "Crocoseum" (an exhibition area at Australia Zoo) and during subsequent media interviews. To lose her closest friend, her soul mate, was heart wrenching. However, on the Universal Waite version of the Ten of Swords, there appears to be a new day dawning— which brings me to the next card.

**Page of Wands:** Bindi Irwin took the baton from her father's hand and is now running with it—at ten years of age! Sharing her father's characteristic charm and enthusiasm, she now stars in the TV show *Bindi: The Jungle Girl*, carrying on the legacy of her father, whom she called her hero. The poise and heartfelt sentiments she expressed at her dad's memorial service were extraordinary to watch. Bindi plunged headlong into taking her father's place, quite on her own. Her optimism and can-do attitude are as infectious as Steve's—which no doubt help comfort Terri during difficult days. This rising star will certainly be a confident, energetic champion of wildlife, just like her beloved daddy.

## COMMENTARY

Notice how some of the cards in the Major Arcana evoke an archetypal picture just by their names. For example, some people considered Steve Irwin a "fool" for dallying with wildlife at such close quarters. And considering his "sleight of hand" way of avoiding dangerous situations (before his death), it can definitely be said that he was a Magician of sorts, especially with his showmanship. The daring of animal tamers in circuses could definitely be a representation of Strength, as could larger-than-life performers who show an internal fortitude that leads them where angels fear to tread.

## YOUR TURN

— Have you ever witnessed an amazing spectacle at a live performance or perhaps on TV? What did you think and feel? Pair your experiences with relevant cards.

— Do you know of someone who has emerged from a tragic situation with grace, and perhaps even spunk and a new lease on life? What happened? Choose the appropriate cards to symbolize the people, events, and feelings associated with situation.

— Can you think of an entertainer who consistently wows the crowd, and perhaps comes under fire at times for their antics? Which cards would you select to represent their persona, costumes or clothes, props, and the public reaction to their behavior?

# 9/11

## Lon Milo DuQuette

The destruction of the twin towers of New York City's World Trade Center on September 11, 2001, was the seminal event of the first decade of the twenty-first century. Theories concerning what really happened abound, and nearly everyone, including me, has an opinion. Here's what I see when I go "back in time" to view that terrible event and its aftermath through the magickal lens of the Tarot.

Deck used: *Thoth Tarot*

**The Moon:** Two figures of the jackal-headed Egyptian god Anubis (guardian of the dead) stand before the dark twin towers of the Moon card. Drops of blood fall from the sky in the space between the two towers. All is not as it appears. Illuminated by the false light of the moon in her infernal aspect, the entire card is a glyph of madness and deception, the nauseating delusion of a nightmare.

**The Tower:** This card is also titled "the Blasted Tower" and "the House of God." The scene is dominated by a lightning-struck tower crumbling in flames as human figures plunge from the heights. The white dove of peace, olive branch still in her beak, soars toward the edge of the card as if to flee the horrible spectacle. (See Joan Bunning's "The Struck Tower" and Lisa Hunt's "The Year of the Tower Card" for their takes on the Tower card in connection with 9/11.)

**Eight of Swords:** This card is also titled "Interference" or "Lord of Shortened Force." Jet fighters that could have intercepted the hijacked commercial planes are unable to assist because they are occupied in an "exercise" that Vice President Dick Cheney ordered and supervised many hundreds of miles away. Chaos on multiple communication levels ensues.

**The Hanged Man:** Television viewers around the world are helpless as they are bound to their sets watching the scenes of horror unfold.

**Five of Disks:** This card is also called "Worry." The large fragmented disks on the card suggest the breach in the wall where a plane or missile penetrates the building. When the Pentagon is hit, the nation worries that the White House will be targeted next.

**Death:** The enormity of the death toll begins to sink in as reports of the buildings' occupancy numbers are calculated. The day has become a grotesque dance of death.

**Ten of Swords:** This card is alternately titled "Ruin." Shortly after Lady Harris painted this card on September 18, 1939, she wrote Aleister Crowley saying, "I have done the Ten of Swords & promptly Russia takes up arms." (For more information on the artist for Crowley's Thoth deck, Lady Frieda Harris, see the commentary for both this BIT Snapshot and for Mark McElroy's "Finding My Way Back to Faith" in chapter 3.)

**The Emperor:** Presidential authority gains near martial-law omnipotence. Congress becomes a rubber stamp to the buildup to war. *Habeas corpus* is suspended. Phones and e-mails of an entire nation are monitored.

## COMMENTARY

In his intriguing book *Understanding Aleister Crowley's Thoth Tarot*, Lon had this to say about the deck he used for his BIT Snapshot, one of the most arresting Tarot decks extant:

> When we ask what makes the Thoth Tarot unique, the first and most obvious answer is the artwork . . . The cards of the Thoth Tarot display more than just Lady Harris's skillful execution of traditional tarot images, fine-tuned to reflect a more modern understanding of self and the natural universe . . . Harris exceeded Crowley's wildest expectations by actually incorporating within the very fabric of her style the profoundly subtle essence of his spiritual doctrine. It was a supreme wedding of artistic technique and deepest mysticism.

Some Tarotists associate the Emperor with the "long arm of the law," as well as all things governmental. On one end of the spectrum, laws can protect individuals and enable a smoothly functioning democracy. Taken to the other extreme, however, laws (or even unauthorized actions) can result in invasion of privacy, abuse of authority, and oppression.

In his book, Lon quotes Aleister Crowley on the Moon card from the *Book of Thoth*: "Upon the hills are black towers of nameless mystery, of horror and of fear. All prejudice, all superstition, dead tradition and ancestral loathing, all combine to darken her face before the eyes of men." Indeed, as 9/11 was occurring, the public watched in helpless horror, not knowing what was happening as plumes of dark smoke rose upward and ash spread across New York City.

In the *Thoth Tarot*, six horizontal swords and two vertical ones form a type of lattice in the Eight of Swords card. Because the swords suit often relates to the realm of communication, the overlying swords almost seem to form a wall—perhaps signifying blocked messages. In fact, in his book, Lon describes the complex Qabalistic and astrological associations with this card, noting, "Jupiter in Gemini indicates an element of luck in intellectual pursuits. Hod is the sphere of Mercury, who rules Gemini. As it does to the eights of the other suits, however, Hod's imbalance and lowly position on the Tree of Life throws a wet blanket on what otherwise might have been a fortunate coupling." If those jet fighters weren't already engaged in military exercises hundreds of miles away, their presence would have indeed been advantageous and, just maybe, could have intercepted the second plane that slammed into the Twin Towers.

In many Tarot decks, the Hanged Man, or Hanged One, is suspended from a tree or post. Most times, he appears content, even radiant. In other images, he appears trussed against his will. In the Thoth Tarot version of the Hanged Man, the figure is suspended upside down, the left leg attached to an ankh via a coiled snake. Phrases such as "hung up," "hang on," "hang tight," "hang ten," "hang in there," or "hung in the air" all imply some type of fixation, cessation, or suspension; and on 9/11, many around the world suspended everyday life as they sat glued to their televisions, in complete shock.

The Death card in the Thoth deck is truly a work of art—sacred geometry, in fact. Technically speaking, it's one of the most striking renderings of the Death card, especially with Lady Harris's painted geometric lines emanating from the crowned ebony skeleton. I'm actually a bit surprised Lon picked the Death card for this BIT Snapshot because I'm familiar with his unusually positive take on this card. He writes:

> The Death card of the Thoth Tarot is the antithesis of those found in traditional packs. This is no stiff grim reaper standing on the Earth, indiscriminately mowing down people, young and old, humble and highborn. This Death is vivacious and flexible. He wears the crown of Osiris and dances madly on the bottom of the sea. Instead of mowing down the living, he uses his scythe to stir up bubbles of new lives from out of the seemingly dead and decaying sediment.

Regarding the Ten of Swords, Lon acknowledges, "It is difficult to put a good spin on this card" because "[a]long with the other tens, the Ten of Swords can't degenerate any lower without completely changing suits." Quoting Crowley, Lon says the creator of the *Thoth Tarot* intended the Ten of Swords to represent the "ruin of the Intellect . . . and even all of mental moral qualities." For eons, humanity has speculated if any "good" can come from violence and war. Just as many lives, families, businesses, and alliances were ruined on 9/11, violence continues to ripple outward from that fateful day.

## YOUR TURN

— The impact of 9/11 was worldwide. Where were *you* when the Twin Towers fell? What were your thoughts and feelings? How has your view of America changed? Your view of the world? Choose cards that represent your attitude, surroundings, and reactions at the time and at present.

— How did your friends, family, co-workers, teachers, or community react to 9/11? Were there blood drives, appeals for donations, or recruitment for volunteers to help at Ground Zero? Which cards do you feel best represent what was going on around you at the time?

— If we are to believe the media, world opinion of the United States has shifted dramatically since 9/11. How do you feel other countries view America? Select cards to represent the actions taken on behalf of the United States, as well as the attitudes and perceptions of the world at large.

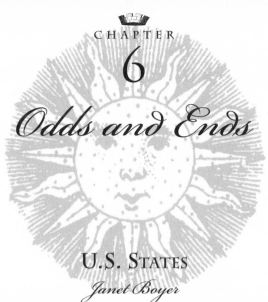

# 6
# Odds and Ends

## U.S. States
### Janet Boyer

Tarot cards can offer us insight into location and destination from the micro to the macro. I once used the *Victorian Romantic Tarot* deck to locate my missing glasses; I found them in an unusual place (on the floor near a doorway), one clearly indicated by the image on the Nine of Wands card!

Location can be helpful when doing readings for others as well. Recently, I did an e-mail reading for a U.S. resident on an extended stay in Mexico. Among her questions was a desirable location for future work. When I pulled the Sun, I immediately thought of a balmy location in the Mediterranean and told her as much. It turns out that she is an accomplished violinist and had a wild dream to play music for a certain hotel in Italy. She had even e-mailed them offering her services. The clincher? The hotel happens to be in a town *right on the Mediterranean!*

As you immerse yourself in Tarot, you'll find that hunches, information, and insight arise from your intuition, as well as from card imagery and symbolism. Once you've handled a particular deck (or decks) for a period of time, you'll remember many of the card images by osmosis. You may eventually be able to do a Tarot reading without cards.

Yes, although it sounds like a wild idea, it is quite possible to "read" without an actual deck. One time I was in a Barnes & Noble bookstore, browsing in the children's section. I approached a woman who I thought was an employee and asked her about recommendations for a children's encyclopedia. As I was asking, however, the thought crossed my mind that maybe she wasn't an employee after all, because she looked like a teacher. I then backpedaled and asked her. Well, she happened to be a veteran schoolteacher *and* a store employee.

We got to talking, and, somehow, writing and Tarot reading entered the conversation. She told me that she'd had a Tarot reading many years ago and would like to get another someday. A card popped into my mind, and I asked her if she wanted a reading right then. (It's customary among ethical readers to get a person's permission before offering any information or performing a reading.) She was thrilled by the prospect, so I began explaining the cards I saw in my mind's eye and explained what I felt they were indicating. One of the cards happened to be the Six of Swords, which often shows individuals in a boat sailing away from choppy waves into calmer water. When this image came to mind, however, I immediately saw a place near the eastern coast of the United States. When I asked her if she planned to move somewhere on the East Coast where there were beaches, her jaw dropped. She and her husband had been looking into property at just such a place.

As you can see, location can be an important part of Tarot readings. I thought it would be a fun exercise to do a BIT Snapshot on the various states, so I got out my son's states and capitals flash cards, discovered fascinating information, and began pairing the states with Tarot cards.

Deck used: *Universal Waite Tarot*

**Three of Pentacles:** *Pennsylvania.* Ah, my beloved home—the Keystone State! The first card that comes to mind when I think of Pennsylvania's nickname is the Three of Pentacles from the Universal Waite deck. In that card, one of the central images is an archway with three encircled five-pointed stars. A worker stands on a bench, tools in hand, speaking with what looks to be a monk and a cloaked individual. The construction of an arch usually involves wedge-shaped stones or bricks, and the central stone is placed at the highest point. Called a keystone, this particular stone or brick holds the others in place.

**Knight of Pentacles:** *Missouri.* According to Microsoft Encarta Encyclopedia 2002, Missouri was known originally as the "Gateway to the West" but gained another nickname in 1899 when Congressman Willard D. Vandiver said, "I come from a country that raises corn and cotton and cockleburs and Democrats, and frothy eloquence neither convinces nor satisfies me. I'm from Missouri. You've got to show me." After that, Missouri was best known as the Show Me State.

When I consider cautious individuals who rely on five-sensory proof over persuasive speech, intuition, or mystical connection, I think of the earth signs of the zodiac: Taurus, Virgo, and Capricorn. In the Minor Arcana, the pentacles suit (in other decks called disks, coins, crystals, or stones) is associated with the element of earth. As I noted in my BIT Snapshot for *Mary Poppins* (see chapter 4), of all the cards among the pentacles, it's the knight I most associate with caution, stubbornness, and skepticism. Just like the spirit of Missouri's nickname, the Knight of Pentacles would, in my estimation, be most likely to live by the motto "seeing is believing."

**The Devil:** *Wyoming.* The 1977 movie *Close Encounters of the Third Kind*, starring Richard Dreyfuss and directed by Steven Spielberg, won an Academy Award and remains a favorite among sci-fi movie enthusiasts. In addition to a haunting five-note musical tone, a mysterious monolith becomes the central focus of the film. That monolith is Devil's Tower, a pillar of molten basalt that appears to have vertical scratches running from top to bottom. (According to Native American legend, these vertical columns were claw marks left by a giant bear.)

Although the devil on this card has claws on his feet and shares its name with Devil's Tower national monument in the Black Hills, I see another interesting correlation between Wyoming and this card: The shape of this state is a perfect rectangle, and if you rotate the shape, it looks just like the black rectangular pillar the devil in the card sits on. Also, Roy Neary, the character played by Dreyfuss in the film, became obsessed with Devil's Tower to the point that it destroyed his personal life (remember the plate of mounded mashed potatoes?). I associate the Devil card with obsession that often leads to some sort of implosion within a personality to the extent of dangerous impulses.

**The Sun:** *Florida.* Although it may seem a no-brainer to assign the Sun to the Sunshine State, I chose this card to represent Florida for other reasons. Besides having a sunny climate and palm trees, Florida is home to one of the most popular vacation destinations in the world: Walt Disney World. (Universal Studios, another large amusement complex, is also in Orlando.) Walter Elias Disney's innovation, playfulness, and fantastical imagination still sparkle throughout the world via the Disney Imagineers (who envision and build the attractions at the parks), beloved characters, and memorable movies.

The companion book to the *DruidCraft Tarot* by Philip and Stephanie Carr-Gomm has this to say about the Sun card: "This is the card of your full creative potential being realized in the world . . . with the brightness, strength, and clarity of God and the sun, and of your expressive powers. The work of the bard as poet, musician, artist, and storyteller is elevated in this card. . . ."

Walt Disney knew how to gather talented individuals to create magic, and his vibrant legacy lives on. Some Tarotists use "Disney" as a curse word to snub whimsical, lighthearted Tarot decks or stories. The Carr-Gomms, however, go on to say this about the Sun: "[W]e are liberated from everyday worries and constraints—we don't care if we appear childlike or 'naked', free of guile or hidden agendas. Instead, we are free to be exactly who we are, and to give to the world exactly what it is that we are supposed to give—what we were born to give."

**The Chariot:** *Alaska.* Known as the Last Frontier, Alaska is the largest state, yet the most sparsely populated. I chose the Chariot to represent the forty-ninth state because of the Iditarod, the grueling annual dog-sledding race commemorating the diphtheria epidemic of 1925. In a race to save the residents of Nome, Alaska, from this contagious disease, dog mushers covered approximately 700 miles to deliver a lifesaving serum.

The Chariot plunges headlong through obstacles toward victory, propelled by single-minded focus, steely courage, and a fierce will—the same type of will that not only fueled the dog mushers in 1925, but also the hardy Iditarod racers of today.

## COMMENTARY

Inspiration for a BIT Snapshot can come from anywhere. In terms of location, including U.S. states, card correlation can be based on border shape, motto, nickname, flag, attractions, food, industries, historical incidents, personal memories, famous (or infamous) residents, annual events, or sporting teams. You're limited only by your imagination.

In his book *The Tarot: A Key to the Wisdom of the Ages*, Paul Foster Case, famed occultist and founder of the esoteric organization Builders of the Adytum (BOTA), attributes the Devil to the earth sign of Capricorn. I chose the Knight of Pentacles to represent the "show me" attitude of the Missouri motto, but Case has this to say about the Devil's connection to reliance on the five senses, as well as to the Hierophant:

The Devil's uplifted right hand has all its fingers open, as if in contradiction to the sign of esotericism made by the Hierophant. The latter's gesture says: "What you see is not all there is to know." The Devil's gesture intimates: "What sensation reports is all there is to it." On the palm of this uplifted hand [in the Case/BOTA deck] is outlined an astrological symbol of the planet Saturn, ruling in Capricorn.

## Your Turn

— With your home state, country, or town in mind (or current residence), which card or cards would you select to represent various aspects of this particular location, including the neighborhood, surroundings, tourist attractions, social groups, organizations, and so on?

— Think of somewhere you've always wanted to visit (or a favorite destination). Which cards would you choose to represent the climate, people, cultural institutions, and history of this place, as well as why you enjoy it so much?

— Recall a landmark, famous attraction, or city where something significant happened in history, a film, a book, or current events. Select cards to represent the environment, culture, and people surrounding this notable situation.

# Songs from the 1980s
### Janet Boyer

Arguably one of the best eras for music, the eighties were a time of big hair, fluorescent colors, leg warmers, upturned collars, stonewashed jeans, and banana hair clips. Madonna began her reign as a pop goddess; synthesizers replaced disco beats, and glam metal found dudes raiding their moms' makeup bags. Surprisingly, some successful acts from the 1980s are still around making music—but they're sporting a lot less hair and mascara.

Deck used: *Universal Waite Tarot*

**Wheel of Fortune:** *"Changes" by Yes.* There's only one constant in life, and that is change. The capricious Wheel seems to dump fortune in one person's lap, while robbing another blind. Some people believe that a petty God lives upstairs, ready to deliver a toasty lightning bolt to those who are bad and luxurious rewards to those who are good. Others believe it is the Law of Attraction serving up whatever a person happens to be "vibrating." One thing is for sure: the Wheel brings frustration and delight, luck and disaster. How you interpret the source of the cycles is entirely up to you.

**The Emperor:** *"Everybody Wants to Rule the World" by Tears for Fears.* Bureaucracy, gridlock, and insane pressure. While many of us don't want to rule the entire world like an emperor might, we certainly want to rule *ours.* What happens when the energy of rules, boundaries, and calling the shots butts up against another's desire to do the same? Compromise would be one solution, but you'll have to look to another card for that . . .

**Seven of Cups:** *"Sweet Dreams (Are Made of This)" by the Eurythmics.* "I've traveled the world and the seven seas—everybody's looking for something." Because of all the intriguing choices offered in each of the seven cups in the imagery, I consider the Seven of Cups to be the "life is a buffet" card. Fame, fortune, identity, knowledge, truth, achievement, love, peace, meaning—yes, just about everyone is chasing after *something.* Every dream, even a crazy one, begins with a healthy dose of imagination, so is it possible that believing is a precursor to seeing?

**Two of Swords:** *"I Know There's Something Going On" by Frida.* Onefourth of the seventies group ABBA, this attractive redheaded Swede, aided by tons of reverb, sang this haunting refrain. More often than not, many individuals do, indeed, know when "something" is going on because they're equipped with gut feelings. Like the blindfolded lady in the Two of Swords, however, they choose to "see no evil" (or refuse to address it), so they go on pretending that *nothing* is going on.

**Ace of Cups:** *"Higher Love" by Steve Winwood.* When I think of the Lovers, arranged marriages and fitting partnerships come to mind. The Two of Cups, for me, is the deep connection of soul mates and close friends. What exactly is a love higher than that? Well, I see the Ace of Cups as a pure heart, communion with the Divine, and unconditional love.

**Five of Pentacles:** *"Jeopardy" by the Greg Kihn Band.* Admittedly, "Weird Al" Yankovic's spoof of this song has tainted my memory a bit ("I was on Jeopardy . . . baby"), but when lead singer Kihn asks, "Where were you when I needed you?" I think of the Five of Pentacles. I can totally see the two huddling figures in the foreground as individuals who helped others in their time of need, only to be abandoned when they were in jeopardy.

**Five of Cups:** *"Tainted Love" by Soft Cell.* Speaking of tainted, I just had to include my absolute favorite song from the eighties! "Take my tears and that's not nearly *alllll*, tainted love . . ." Although the tossing, turning, and not sleeping at night would be more akin to Nine of Swords, I've always gotten a weird vibe from the Five of Cups. The figure cloaked in black—what's going on behind the robe? Every time I look at the Universal Waite version of this card, I could swear the figure is peeking above the cloak to see if anyone feels sorry for him. "Boo hoo. My feelings are hurt." Call me cynical, but I suspect they're crocodile tears, and if that's the case, there's probably a manipulator under that cloak. "Once I ran to you, now I run from you." Indeed!

**Six of Cups:** *"Don't You (Forget about Me)" by Simple Minds.* In one Tarot tradition, the Six of Cups is associated with the sun in Scorpio. One thing is certain about Scorpios, especially low-level ones: They never forget—

particularly injuries and slights. This lovely croon tune refers, however, to looking to the past with fondness and longing, another meaning often associated with this card. "Hey, hey, hey, hey . . ."

**Ten of Pentacles:** *"Our House" by Madness.* "Mother wearing her Sunday best"—never a good sign in song or movies. Oh, it sounds so 1950s perfect, but behind closed doors, there's probably spousal abuse, child neglect, Internet-porn addiction, and alcoholism. But golly, I bet the linoleum floor sparkles! If the Ten of Cups is the truly cohesive, loving family, then the Ten of Pentacles may very well be the ones who pretend to be such because for them, appearances are *everything.*

**Four of Cups:** *"I Don't Care Anymore" by Phil Collins.* Whether jaded by experience or disappointed by expectations, the bored-looking figure in the Universal Waite version of this card seems to exude an "I just don't care" attitude. Like the lyrics of this song, he just sits there "and bides his time." But what is it that he's waiting for? A hand emerges from the cloud, bearing a cup—what might that represent to the central figure in this card? We can only speculate, but his obstinate body language seems to indicate that he needs to deal with whatever is in those three cups before him in order to be open to the offered chalice floating in the air.

**Temperance:** *"Send Me an Angel" by Real Life.* I admit it: I made this choice because I saw it in a dream. No, I'm totally serious. I woke up one day, the dream world trailing ether as it went back from whence it came. In my head, I heard this song and saw the Universal Waite version of Temperance. The lead singer pleads, "Don't give up . . . don't give up . . . I've never been lucky in love." Well, I believe in healing and wishes, so let's hope that angel in the card Temperance brings some measure of peace to the troubled waters of lonely hearts everywhere.

**The Devil:** *"Witch Hunt" by RUSH.* "Quick to judge, quick to anger, slow to understand. Ignorance and prejudice, as we walk hand in hand." The Devil

can be an ignorant SOB—quick to call "evil" what he doesn't know or understand. Or maybe it's as Paul Foster Case noted: "The Devil is God, and He
is misunderstood by the wicked." In any case, if the Devil could truly see
beyond superficial appearances, he'd realize that we're far more similar
than different at core.

## COMMENTARY

Songs convey stories, emotional content, concepts, and messages, which
make them perfect catalysts for stimulating memories and intuition. Symbols
are shortcuts, and like the Tarot, songs are often full of them. Thus, both can
deliver a wide range of information for those who are paying attention.

In the mid-1980s, "totally" was an oft-used term originating with the "Valley
Girls" on the West Coast, but it eventually worked through the entire United
States. (Don't believe me? Look up the lyrics of the song "Valley Girl" by Frank
and Moon Unit Zappa. Yes, Moon Unit is her real name. If that's not bad
enough, she has a brother named Dweezil!) Like, anyway, I'm still not done
with the word "totally," so please excuse the multiple uses in this particular
BIT Snapshot. I'm not trying to gag you with a spoon—honestly.

## YOUR TURN

— Make a list of your favorite songs. Consider the lyrics and beat, as well as
   any memories or emotions evoked. Which cards would you choose to
   pair with the associations that arise?

— Eras and cultures often have distinct musical flavors—from medieval
   chants to doo-wop, surf music to klezmer, and so on. Bring to mind a
   particular culture, era, or style of music and come up with some specific
   songs or tracks. Then go through a Tarot deck and select cards that you
   feel represent those songs.

— Recall a famous singer who made history, went far past their fifteen minutes of fame, or often landed in the headlines. Which cards seem to embody their personality, songs, reputation, and personal life?

## HOLIDAYS, DATES, AND CELEBRATIONS
### *Janet Boyer*

Significant dates can be a wellspring of memories about people, places, and conversations, making them a great backdrop for BIT Snapshots. Seeking insight into important commemorations and milestones can also increase your network of card associations, which will aid your work with the Tarot. Here are a few common holidays and celebrations that I came up with for my BIT Snapshot.

Deck used: *Universal Waite Tarot*, plus one card from the *Oracle Tarot*

**Ace of Swords:** *New Year's Day.* A fresh start and the hope of "the best year ever" often give way to resolutions and goal setting. The firm resolve and bright ideas of the Ace of Swords, however, often stay in the realm of mere potential unless coupled with consistent action. Because it is depicted as a solitary sword, gleaming with promise, I tend to associate the Ace of Swords with new, exciting ideas while the firm grip of the hand reminds me of resolutions.

**Wheel of Fortune:** *St. Patrick's Day.* Amid green beer, bagpipe parades, and corned beef with cabbage, North American revelers clothed in green pay homage to Ireland's patron saint on March 17. Although the holiday is now largely secular, legend has it that St. Patrick used the three-leaf clover to explain the doctrine of the Christian Trinity to the Irish people. In astrology, Jupiter is known as the planet of luck, and one esoteric attribution connects it to the Wheel of Fortune. Because the shamrock is virtually synonymous with the luck of the Irish, this card popped into my mind as the perfect representation of this festive day.

**Justice:** *Tax Day.* Unless one is expecting a refund, April 15 tends to be a dreaded day of reckoning. If you do your own taxes (as I do), keeping track of paperwork throughout the year makes the job easier at tax time, although all the bureaucratic red tape legislated by the Emperor still makes doing taxes a daunting, laborious, and tedious chore. While I see the Emperor as instigating and formulating laws, I view Justice as the actual representation of those laws, as well as law enforcement and what citizens must do to stay on the right side of the blind scales.

**The Empress** and **the Hanged Man:** *Easter.* Unbeknownst to some, Easter has its roots in a pagan holiday honoring the Teutonic goddess, Eastre. Held during the vernal equinox, the annual festival commemorated this goddess of fertility and spring. *Eastre* means "to shine." Both eggs and bunnies became associated with this celebration because of their connection to fertility. On the Empress card of many Tarot decks, a pregnant woman sits amid lush surroundings, including sheaves of grain, opulent fabrics, and luxurious pillows. Indicating creativity, productivity, pregnancy, motherhood, domesticity, and nurturing, this card seems a perfect match for the pre-Christian festival.

For Christians, Easter commemorates the resurrection of Christ. Most Christian theologians believe that the ignominious death by crucifixion, often reserved for criminals, symbolizes Christ's vicarious atonement for the "original sin" of humanity. Because the Hanged Man is suspended from a tree, similar to Jesus Christ hanging on the cross, I often think of the Hanged Man as representing great sacrifice or martyrdom—a central theology of Christianity based on the death of Jesus. Interestingly, Christian teachings hold that the apostle Peter felt unworthy to die in the same manner as Jesus

Christ (perhaps because of the self-reproach he felt at denying his Lord three times), so he requested to be crucified upside down.

**Ten of Pentacles:** *Family reunions.* Often held in the summer when children are out of school and after parents have taken their vacations, family reunions herald a time when several generations gather together to celebrate. Some individuals do extensive genealogical research and share their findings at family reunions. Others bring old photos for reminiscing, while others stand by, camera ready, to snap candid pictures.

My mom is one of thirteen kids and my dad's mom was one of ten children, so family reunions on both sides of my family tend to be quite large. The reunions on my father's side tend to be laid-back affairs, featuring games for children, bingo, a potluck dinner, raffles, giveaways, and an auction. Reunions on my mother's side tend to be more boisterous, with a pig roast, drinking, karaoke, dancing, laughter, a bonfire, a potluck dinner, volleyball, horseshoes, ladder ball, a barbecue on an open pit—and more drinking.

I see the Ten of Pentacles as involving multigenerational issues, including legacies, inheritance, genealogy, and family reunions, especially since the Universal Waite version shows what looks to be an elderly man, a middle-aged woman, a young man, and a child (as well as two dogs).

**The Hierophant:** *Christenings and bar/bat mitzvahs.* In the Universal Waite deck, two individuals kneel or stand before an elevated religious figure who wears a crown. Many believe the central figure is a representation of the pope and that the two individuals in the foreground are probably monks. Seeing the main figure's hand held up in blessing, I think of religious rites of passage that welcome children into a spiritual community or mark their transition into spiritual maturity and responsibilities. Other public rites, such as marriages, crone ceremonies, and death traditions also remind me of the Hierophant's realm.

**Three of Cups:** *Births.* To quote the 1980s *Schoolhouse Rock* song, "A man and a woman had a little baby—three is a magic number." The intimacy suggested by the man and woman in the Two of Cups may lead to an act of creation that could beget a third little cup (or bundle of joy). Also a card of celebration, the Three of Cups, with its three happy, dancing figures, seems a perfect representation for both births and baby showers. (And, let's face it, the majority of baby showers are attended by women, and the Three of Cups card in most decks shows women having a good time.)

**Nine of Wands:** *Veterans Day.* Formerly known as Armistice Day, Veterans Day honors those who have served in U.S. armed forces in wartime. In the Universal Waite deck, an individual with a bandaged head leans on one of the nine staves, looking quite weary. I tend to see the figure on this card as one who wants to stop fighting or who has suffered much in the act of protecting or defending. War is hell, and what soldiers and their families suffer can be unimaginable to civilians. The treatment of Vietnam vets was a travesty (no matter what one's attitude toward the war itself), and many are still homeless on American streets, sometimes suffering from mental illness and posttraumatic stress disorder (PTSD). It would seem that America has learned its lesson, for although most Vietnam vets sadly went the way of the Five of Pentacles, most individuals now support the troops (despite their views on a particular war), giving them the Six of Wands heroes' welcome upon their return.

**Ace of Pentacles:** *Thanksgiving.* I view this card as the feeling of perfect contentment in the moment, a state of gratitude independent of external trappings or measurements of success. Although each person has the potential to tap into a deep well of thankfulness, whether they do so or not is a matter of choice and perhaps temperament. If I were to come up with a phrase to encapsulate this card's attribute, I'd say it's a card of

"I am enough" or "I have enough." For me, the Ace of Pentacles embodies a fullness that doesn't feel it needs more of anything to be complete, which is what I associate with the spirit of Thanksgiving. It's a time of counting blessings, as well as an attitude of always scouting for them. These associations have little to do with the card's image; rather, they come from my emotional connection with the card.

**The Chariot:** *Black Friday.* In the Oracle Tarot, the Chariot card shows a sassy, high-heeled woman striding purposefully behind a cart. Yes, this woman is *shopping!* (And the ladies say, "Woo hoo!") Black Friday is the day after Thanksgiving when insane women (well, mostly women) fight insane crowds attempting to get insane bargains during insane time restrictions. Oh yes, bargains are to be had—but you have to get up at 3:00 a.m., find a parking space, wrestle gals as determined as you, and avoid getting punched, stampeded, or seeing the dreaded message of "insufficient funds." Ack! Not my idea of a good time, but there's no question that to be a retail warrior on Black Friday requires strong resolve, clear-eyed focus, and stamina—just like the woman in the *Oracle Tarot*'s Chariot. (Picking a shopping cart without a squeaky or bent wheel is always a bonus, too, but determined gals corral such pesky irritants much like the charioteer in the Sharman-Caselli deck reins in those two wild-looking horses!)

**The Star:** *Christmas.* Several Tarot decks portray Christmas scenes among a few cards. For example, the Nine of Cups from the *Housewives Tarot* shows a couple opening presents by a Christmas tree. The Nine of Crystals from the *Inner Child Cards* shows a pregnant gnome reading by candlelight next to a decorated tree on Christmas Eve (with nine red stockings hanging above the fireplace among nine glowing candles). The Ten of Crystals from the same deck shows Mama Gnome holding the newborn baby (and hanging up a tenth stocking), while gnome children are opening presents and Papa

Gnome lights the Yule log. The Guide of Crystals (comparable to the Queen of Pentacles in most decks) from the *Inner Child Cards* is St. Nicholas, while Santa Claus/Father Winter makes an appearance as the Emperor in the *Whimsical Tarot* deck.

The card that I associate most with Christmas is the Star. According to the Bible story, the Star of Bethlehem (also know as the Magi's Star) heralded Christ's birth and guided the three wise men to the inn. In the New Testament book of II Peter, Jesus is called the "day star" (Greek: *phosphoros*), while in Revelation he's called the "morning star."

According to the Microsoft Encarta Encyclopedia 2002, Martin Luther was walking through a forest one Christmas Eve and became so deeply moved by the beauty of all the starlit fir trees that he took one indoors and lit it with candles to remind his children of God's creation.

The central symbol of Christmas in our home is a seven-and-a-half-foot tree that we decorate with more than a thousand white lights, accentuated by gold, burgundy, white, and clear ornaments, pearlescent strands of beads, a sparkling antique white garland, and bows of gold lamé and burgundy velvet. A lighted angel of white and gold sits atop this shining wonder. I love shutting off all the lights downstairs and staring at the twinkling Christmas tree. All of the glimmering points of white light, especially as they reflect on and through the ornaments, remind me of a clear, starlit night.

I love stars anyway, especially the constellation Orion. I used to wish upon stars as a child, so the concept of stars fills me with wonder, hope, and joy. They seem to represent possibilities, doorways to new ways of being and seeing. Of course, as Christmas approaches, children hope that they get what's on their lists. Random acts of kindness may very well become stars of hope to a discouraged, despairing individual, igniting a beacon of hope within. This star—humanity's ability to transcend differences, reach out to others, offer a smile, and live out the wish "Peace on Earth, goodwill toward men"—warms my soul during Christmas.

## COMMENTARY

I also see the Nine of Wands card as representing anyone who gives of himself or herself on a consistent basis, such as the patient parent of a disabled child or the spouse of someone who is chronically ill. There are "walking wounded" all over the world who have suffered—and are suffering—their own private wars. As a result, I also associate this card with weariness, physical fatigue, and someone who has been through quite a few battles.

As mentioned in the introduction, deck creators often take liberties with more common court card assignations. In the *Inner Child Cards* deck, children correspond to the pages, seekers to the knights, guides to the queens, and guardians to the kings.

## YOUR TURN

— Recall your favorite holiday, vacation, or celebration. What made it so enjoyable? Select cards to represent who was there, where you were, and why it meant so much to you.

— Is there a holiday or date that others commemorate, but that you just can't seem to understand, much less celebrate? Why do you think that is? Which cards do you feel symbolize your thoughts, feelings, and attitude?

— In school, we're often encouraged to memorize important dates and time periods from history. Think of one of those dates or occasions you had to learn and choose cards to represent the people, places, and events involved.

# The Cards of the Universal Waite

THE FOOL

THE MAGICIAN

THE HIGH PRIESTESS

THE EMPRESS

THE EMPEROR

THE HIEROPHANT

The Lovers

The Chariot

Strength

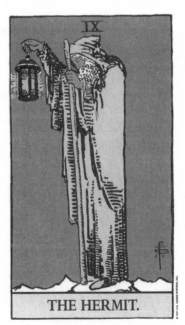

The Hermit

WHEEL of FORTUNE.

JUSTICE.

THE HANGED MAN.

DEATH.

TEMPERANCE

THE DEVIL

THE TOWER

THE STAR

THE MOON

THE SUN

JUDGEMENT

THE WORLD

ACE OF WANDS

TWO OF WANDS

THREE OF WANDS

FOUR OF WANDS

FIVE OF WANDS

SIX OF WANDS

SEVEN OF WANDS

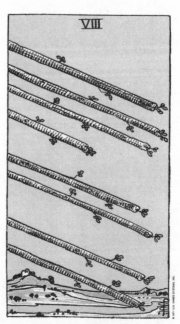

EIGHT OF WANDS

NINE OF WANDS

TEN OF WANDS

PAGE OF WANDS

KNIGHT OF WANDS

QUEEN OF WANDS

KING OF WANDS

ACE OF CUPS

TWO OF CUPS

THREE OF CUPS

FOUR OF CUPS

FIVE OF CUPS

SIX OF CUPS

SEVEN OF CUPS

EIGHT OF CUPS

NINE OF CUPS

TEN OF CUPS

PAGE OF CUPS

KNIGHT OF CUPS

QUEEN OF CUPS

KING OF CUPS

ACE OF SWORDS

TWO OF SWORDS

THREE OF SWORDS

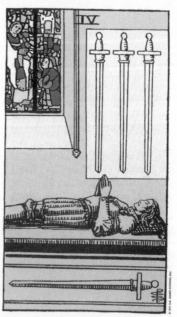

FOUR OF SWORDS

FIVE OF SWORDS

SIX OF SWORDS

SEVEN OF SWORDS

EIGHT OF SWORDS

NINE OF SWORDS

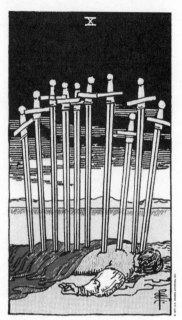

TEN OF SWORDS

PAGE OF SWORDS

KNIGHT OF SWORDS

QUEEN OF SWORDS

KING OF SWORDS

ACE OF PENTACLES

TWO OF PENTACLES

THREE OF PENTACLES

FOUR OF PENTACLES

FIVE OF PENTACLES

SIX OF PENTACLES

SEVEN OF PENTACLES

EIGHT OF PENTACLES

NINE OF PENTACLES

TEN OF PENTACLES

PAGE OF PENTACLES

KNIGHT OF PENTACLES

QUEEN OF PENTACLES

KING OF PENTACLES

# Bibliography

## References

Amberstone, Ruth Ann and Wald. *Tarot Tips*. St. Paul, MN: Llewellyn, 2003.

Andersen, Hans Christian. *The Complete Fairy Tales and Stories.* Translated from the Danish by Erik Christian Haugaard. Garden City, NY: Anchor Books, 1983.

Baum, L. Frank. *The Wonderful Wizard of Oz: 100th Anniversary Edition.* New York: HarperCollins, 2000.

Bunning, Joan. *Learning Tarot Reversals.* Boston: Weiser Books, 2003.

———. *Learning the Tarot.* Boston: Weiser Books, 1998.

Carr-Gomm, Philip and Stephanie, and Will Worthington. *DruidCraft Tarot Companion Book.* New York: St. Martin's Press, 2004.

Case, Paul Foster. *The Tarot: A Key to the Wisdom of the Ages.* New York: Tarcher/Penguin, 2006.

Clayton, Jo. *Changer's Moon.* New York: DAW Books, 1985.

Crowley, Aleister. *Book of Thoth.* York Beach, ME: Weiser Books, 1974.

Cunningham, Elizabeth. *Magdalen Rising.* Rhinebeck, NY: Monkfish, 2007.

———. *The Passion of Mary Magdalen.* Rhinebeck, NY: Monkfish, 2006.

De Angeles, Ly. *Tarot Theory & Practice.* Woodbury, MN: Llewellyn, 2007.

Douglas, John, and Johnny Dodd. *Inside the Mind of BTK*. San Francisco: Jossey-Bass, 2007.

DuQuette, Lon Milo. *Understanding Aleister Crowley's Thoth Tarot*. Boston: Weiser Books, 2003.

Fairfield, Gail. *Everyday Tarot*. Boston: Weiser Books, 2002.

Farber, Monte, and Amy Zerner. *The Instant Tarot Reader*. New York: St. Martin's Press, 1997.

Gawain, Shakti. *Developing Intuition*. Novato, CA: New World Library, 2001.

Gray, Eden. *Tarot Revealed*. New York: Signet, 1969.

Greer, Mary K. *The Complete Book of Tarot Reversals*. St. Paul, MN: Llewellyn, 2002.

———. *Mary K. Greer's 21 Ways to Read a Tarot Card*. Woodbury, MN: Llewellyn, 2006.

Grimm, Jacob and Wilhelm. *Grimm's Fairy Tales*. New York: Barnes & Noble Classics, 2003.

Hayford, Jack, ed. *Spirit Filled Life Bible: New King James Version*. Nashville, TN: Thomas Nelson, 1991.

Katie, Byron. *Loving What Is*. New York: Harmony Books, 2002.

Louis, Anthony. *Tarot Plain and Simple*. St. Paul, MN: Llewellyn, 1996.

MacGregor, Trish, and Phyllis Vega. *Power Tarot*. New York: Fireside Books, 1998.

McElroy, Mark. *Absolute Beginner's Guide to Tarot*. Indianapolis, IN: Que Publishing, 2006.

McPherson, Stephanie Sammartino. *Alexander Graham Bell*. Minneapolis, MN: Lerner Publications, 2007.

Michelsen, Teresa C. *The Complete Tarot Reader*. St. Paul, MN: Llewellyn, 2005.

Myss, Caroline. *Sacred Contracts.* New York: Harmony Books, 2001.

Newton, Michael. *Destiny of Souls.* St. Paul, MN: Llewellyn, 2000.

———. *Journey of Souls.* St. Paul, MN: Llewellyn, 1994.

Nichols, Sallie. *Jung and Tarot: An Archetypal Journey.* New York: Samuel Weiser, 1980.

Ohotto, Robert. *Transforming Fate into Destiny.* Carlsbad, CA: Hay House, 2008.

Pearson, Carol S., and Hugh K. Marr. *What Story Are You Living?* Gainesville, FL: Center for Applications of Psychological Type, 2007.

Pelzer, David. *A Child Called "It": One Child's Courage to Survive.* Deerfield Beach, FL: Health Communications, 1995.

Place, Robert M. *The Tarot: History, Symbolism, and Divination.* New York: Tarcher/Penguin, 2005.

Schwartz, Robert. *Courageous Souls.* N.p.: Whispering Winds Press, 2007.

Sim, Valerie. *Tarot outside the Box.* St. Paul, MN: Llewellyn, 2004.

Steinbeck, John. *Of Mice and Men.* New York: Bantam, 1981.

Sterling, Stephen. *Tarot Awareness.* St. Paul, MN: Llewellyn, 2000.

Stewart, Pete. *The Spiritual Science of the Stars.* Rochester, VT: Inner Traditions, 2007.

Thomson, Sandra. *Pictures from the Heart: A Tarot Dictionary.* New York: St. Martin's Press, 2003.

Tolle, Eckhart. *The Power of Now.* Novato, CA: New World Library, 1999.

Trend Enterprises. *States and Capitals Flash Cards.* St. Paul, MN: Trend Enterprises, 2001.

Vega, Phyllis. *Romancing the Tarot.* New York: Fireside, 2001.

Walsch, Neale Donald. *What God Wants.* New York: Atria Books, 2005.

Wikipedia: "Steve Irwin." http://en.wikipedia.org/wiki/Steve_Irwin.

# ADDITIONAL RECOMMENDED BOOKS

Alligo, Pietro. *Twenty Years of Tarot: The Lo Scarabeo Story.* Torino, Italy: Lo Scarabeo, 2007.

Braden, Nina Lee. *Tarot for Self Discovery.* St. Paul, MN: Llewellyn, 2002.

Carroll, Wilma. *The 2-Hour Tarot Tutor.* New York: Berkley Books, 2004.

Ellershaw, Josephine, and Ciro Marchetti. *Easy Tarot: Learn to Read the Cards Once and for All!* (featuring the *Gilded Tarot*). St. Paul, MN: Llewellyn, 2007.

Greer, Mary K., and Tom Little. *Understanding the Tarot Court.* St. Paul, MN: Llewellyn, 2004.

Gwain, Rose. *Discovering Your Self through the Tarot: A Jungian Guide to Archetypes and Personality.* Rochester, VT: Destiny Books, 1994.

Kaplan, Stuart, and Jane Huets. *The Encyclopedia of Tarot: Vol. IV.* Stamford, CT: U.S. Games Systems, 2005.

McElroy, Mark. *Bright Idea Deck/Book Kit.* St. Paul, MN: Llewellyn, 2005.

———. *What's in the Cards for You?* St. Paul, MN: Llewellyn, 2005.

Ricklef, James. *Tarot Tells the Tale.* St. Paul, MN: Llewellyn, 2003.

Sharman-Burke, Juliet. *Beginner's Guide to Tarot.* New York: St. Martin's Griffin, 2001.

Warwick-Smith, Kate. *The Tarot Court Cards.* Rochester, VT: Destiny Books, 2003.

Woolfolk, Joanna Martine. *The Only Astrology Book You'll Ever Need.* Lanham, MD: Madison Books, 2001.

# Tarot Decks Referenced in This Book

*Albano-Waite Tarot* by Frankie Albano (U.S. Games Systems)

*Animals Divine Tarot* by Lisa Hunt (Llewellyn)

*Baroque Bohemian Cats' Tarot* by Karen Mahony and Alex Ukolov
(Magic Realist Press)

*Bright Idea Deck* by Mark McElroy and Eric Hotz (Llewellyn)

*Celtic Wisdom Tarot* by Caitlín Matthews and Olivia Rayner
(Destiny Books)

*DruidCraft Tarot* by Philip and Stephanie Carr-Gomm; Will Worthington
(St. Martin's Press)

*Etruscan Tarot* by Riccardo Minetti (Lo Scarabeo)

*Fantastical Creatures Tarot* by D. J. Conway and Lisa Hunt
(U.S. Games Systems)

*Ferret Tarot* by Elaine Moertl (self-published)

*Gilded Tarot* by Ciro Marchetti (Llewellyn); comes as part of a boxed set
with Josephine Ellershaw's book *Easy Tarot: Learn to Read the Cards
Once and for All!*

*Gill Tarot* by Elizabeth Josephine Gill (U.S. Games Systems)

*Golden Dawn Ritual Tarot* by Chic and Sandra Tabatha Cicero (Llewellyn)

*Golden Tarot* by Kat Black (U.S. Games Systems)

*Halloween Tarot* by Kipling West and Karin Lee (U.S. Games Systems)

*Hanson-Roberts Tarot* by Mary Hanson-Roberts (U.S. Games Systems)

*Housewives Tarot* by Paul Kepple and Jude Buffum (Quirk Books)

*Hudes Tarot* by Susan Hudes (U.S. Games Systems)

*Inner Child Cards* by Isha Lerner, Mark Lerner, and Christopher Guilfoil
(Bear & Company)

*Jean Noblet Tarot* by Jean-Claude Flornoy (self-published)

*Lisa Hunt Fairytale Tarot* by Lisa Hunt (Llewellyn)

*Llewellyn Tarot* by Anna Marie Ferguson (Llewellyn)

*Lo Scarabeo Tarot* by Mark McElroy and Anna Lazzarini (Lo Scarabeo)

*Morgan-Greer Tarot* by Bill F. Greer and Lloyd Morgan
   (U.S. Games Systems)

*Motherpeace Tarot* by Vicki Noble and Karen Vogel (U.S. Games Systems)

*Mystic Faerie Tarot* by Barbara Moore and Linda Ravenscroft (Llewellyn)

*Oracle Tarot* by Lucy Cavendish and Melinda Ayre (Hay House)

*Osho Zen Tarot* by Osho and Deva Padma (St. Martin's Press)

*Pictorial Key Tarot* by Davide Corsi (Lo Scarabeo)

*Quest Tarot* by Joseph Ernest Martin (Llewellyn)

*Renaissance Tarot* by Brian Williams (U.S. Games Systems)

*Revelations Tarot* by Zach Wong (Llewellyn)

*Rider-Waite Tarot Deck* by Arthur Edward Waite and
   Pamela Colman Smith (U.S. Games Systems)

*Robin Wood Tarot* by Robin Wood (Llewellyn)

*Sacred Rose Tarot* by Johanna Gargiulo-Sherman (U.S. Games Systems)

*Sharman-Caselli Tarot* by Juliet Sharman-Burke and Giovanni Caselli
   (St. Martin's Griffin)

*Tarot of Dreams* by Ciro Marchetti (self-published)

*Tarot of Oz* by David Sexton (Llewellyn)

*Thoth Tarot* by Aleister Crowley and Lady Frieda Harris (Weiser)

*Transformational Tarot* by Arnell Ando (U.S. Games Systems)

*True Love Tarot* by Amy Zerner and Monte Farber (St. Martin's Press)

*Universal Waite Tarot* by Arthur Edward Waite and Pamela Colman Smith, colored by Mary Hanson-Roberts (U.S. Games Systems)

*Vanessa Tarot* by Lynyrd Narciso (U.S. Games Systems)

*Victorian Romantic Tarot* by Karen Mahony and Alex Ukolov (Magic Realist Press)

*Voyager Tarot* by James Wanless (Fair Winds Press)

*Wheel of Change Tarot* by Alexandra Genetti (Destiny Books)

*Whimsical Tarot* by Dorothy Morrison and Mary Hanson-Roberts (U.S. Games Systems)

*World Spirit Tarot* by Lauren O'Leary and Jessica Godino (Llewellyn)

*WorldTree Tarot* by Ann Cass (WorldTree Products)

# About the Contributing Authors and Artists

**J**anet Boyer loves learning, books, autumn, chocolate, trees, coffee, mysteries, thriller movies, the progressive rock band RUSH, and her Tanjberry Library. She adores the Ten of Cups life that she shares with her precious husband and son (whom she home-schools) and their two fur balls. In addition to authoring *The Back in Time Tarot Book* and creating the BIT Method, Janet is a prolific writer and reviewer, having posted more than one thousand reviews and articles to JanetBoyer.com, Amazon.com, and elsewhere. She is the editor of the *2009 Tarot World Annual* (TWM Publishing), as well as the reviews editor at *Tarot World Magazine* and an editor at TheTarotChannel.com. And as if that weren't enough, she also performs intuitive Tarot readings for her worldwide clientele via email through her Web site JanetBoyer.com. To read freshly brewed BIT Snapshots using her innovative Back in Time Method, check out Janet's column in the quarterly print publication *Tarot World Magazine*.

**Nina Lee Braden,** author of *Tarot for Self Discovery* (Llewellyn), lives and teaches in Tennessee. She is the founder of 78 Faces of Divinity, a spiritual group based on Tarot and astrology. She is also a member of the Ancient Order of Druids in America.

**Joan Bunning** is the author of *Learning the Tarot, Learning Tarot Reversals*, and *Learning Tarot Spreads* (all from Weiser). Since 1995, she has maintained her Web site, Learning the Tarot (www.learntarot.com), for the online community.

**Wilma Carroll** is the author of the *2-Hour Tarot Tutor* (Berkley) and has been a practicing intuitive consultant for more than thirty-five years. She has appeared on *Live with Regis and Kelly, The Late Show with David Letterman*, the Learning Channel (TLC), and Telemundo, as well as *Fox News* and *Good Day New York*. She has also been featured in the *Daily News, New York Post, Teen People, Vibe*, and the *New York Observer*. She invites you to visit her Web site, www.wilmacarroll.com.

**Ann Cass** has been reading Tarot since around 1974 and the slightly drunken aftermath of a Society for Creative Anachronism event. For the next twenty years, based on the principle "don't fix it if it ain't broke," she resisted learning anything about the cards except what came in by osmosis. When she started actually putting a deck together, she gave in (to a certain extent) and actually spent some time finding out what a Tarot deck "ought" to be. Ann has been a mechanical engineer, a programmer and computer geek, horse trainer, songwriter, Web designer, and graphic artist. She's currently working at making a new house livable, getting all her computers set up properly, and getting back to doing artwork.

**Elizabeth Cunningham** is a poet and novelist based in New York. Her latest collection of poetry is *Wild Mercy: Tarot-Inspired Musings*. She is the author of the Maeve Chronicles, a series of novels featuring the feisty Celtic

Mary Magdalen. To learn more about her work, you can visit Elizabeth's Web site at www.passionofmarymagdalen.com.

**Lon Milo DuQuette** is the author of fourteen critically acclaimed books (translated into nine languages) on magick and the occult, and he is one of the most respected and entertaining writers and lecturers in the field of Western Hermeticism. Since 1975 he has been a national and international governing officer of Ordo Templi Orientis, one of the most influential magickal societies of the twentieth century. He is an internationally recognized authority on Tarot and western ceremonial magick. Although he takes these subjects very seriously, he tries not to take himself too seriously. This rare combination of scholarship and humor has earned him, over the past twenty years, a unique and respected position in American spiritual and esoteric literature. He is a faculty member of the Omega Institute in Rhinebeck, New York, and at Robert Anton Wilson's Maybe Logic Academy. He lives in Costa Mesa, California, with Constance, his wife of forty years.

**Josephine Ellershaw** is the author of *Easy Tarot: Learn to Read the Cards Once and for All!*, featuring Ciro Marchetti's *Gilded Tarot* (Llewellyn). Professionally, she has many years experience providing readings, coaching, healing, personal development, and metaphysical guidance to an international clientele. Her services are available through her Web site, the Tarot Technique (www.learn-tarot-cards.com). Along with her spiritual work, she owns and runs a health club and a property-development business. She lives in North Yorkshire, England, with her family and large menagerie of pets, including waifs, strays, and rescues.

**Mary K. Greer** is a revolutionary, breaking all the rules regarding methods of learning and using Tarot cards. She has forty years of Tarot experience and, as an author and teacher, emphasizes personal insight and creativity. As a Tarot reader, she works as a "midwife of the soul," using techniques that are interactive, transformational, and empowering. Mary is a member of numerous Tarot organizations and is featured at Tarot conferences and symposia around the world. She is the proud recipient of the 2007 International Tarot Lifetime Achievement award. The author of eight books on Tarot and a biography of four female magicians, her latest book is *Mary K. Greer's 21 Ways to Read a Tarot Card* (Llewellyn).

**Lisa Hunt** is a watercolorist who has spent her life exploring how art can serve as a vehicle for communicating ideas, feelings, and imagery contained within the psyche. She is the artist for several Tarot decks and is the author/artist of the acclaimed *Animals Divine Tarot* (Llewellyn), which won a 2006 COVR award and was voted a top ten Tarot deck of 2005 by Aeclectic Tarot. In 2007, her *Fantastical Creatures Tarot* (U.S. Games) was also voted a top ten Tarot deck by Aeclectic for that year. Her most recent deck is the *Lisa Hunt Fairytale Tarot* (Llewellyn). Lisa earned a master's degree in interdisciplinary studies with an emphasis on Jungian psychology/art and drawing. She enjoys reading, researching, sketching, and writing as a way of feeding her creative soul. She lives with her husband, photographer Kort Kramer, and their family in Florida. You can learn more about Lisa and her work by visiting her Web sites: the Art of Lisa Hunt (www.lisahuntart.com), Animals Divine Tarot (www.animalsdivine.com), and Fantastical Creatures Tarot (www.fantasticalcreatures.com).

**Mark McElroy** is editor-in-chief of the Tarot Channel (www.thetarot channel.com). In addition to writing on every topic from Apple computers to dream control, he is the creator of the *Bright Idea Deck* (Llewellyn), a powerful, flexible brainstorming tool disguised as a pack of cards (and based on the Tarot). As a Tarot and I Ching expert, Mark has contributed material for Tarot-related segments on radio and television shows (including ABC-TV's *Who Wants to Be a Millionaire*) and articles in newspapers. His best-selling book so far, the *Absolute Beginner's Guide to Tarot* (Que Publishing), strips away spookiness, positioning the cards as powerful tools for brainstorming and personal insight. Mark is based in Atlanta, Georgia, but travels frequently. His latest credits include the *Tarot of the Elves* and the *Lo Scarabeo Tarot*, both from the renowned Italian publishers Lo Scarabeo.

**Teresa Michelsen** is a Tarot reader, author, and teacher with more than twenty-five years of experience reading Tarot. Well known on Tarot e-mail discussion lists, she has published many articles on Tarot on the Web. Teresa is the author of two Tarot books, *Designing Your Own Tarot Spreads* and *The Complete Tarot Reader*, both published by Llewellyn. She lives near Seattle, Washington, and, in addition to her Tarot work, has home-based businesses in environmental consulting and mediation. You can visit her award-winning Web site Tarot Moon at www.tarotmoon.com.

**Riccardo Minetti** is an editor, graphic designer, and computer specialist at the renowned Italian publisher Lo Scarabeo. He is the author of the *Etruscan Tarot, Manga Tarot*, and other decks.

**Phyllis Vega** is a practicing astrologer and Tarot reader and has been a New Age counselor for more than three decades. She is the author of nine books: *Lovestrology* (Fair Winds); *What Your Birthday Reveals about You* (Fair Winds); *Sydney Omarr's Sun, Moon, and You* (Signet); *Your Magickal Name*, coauthored with Debra Vega (New Page); *Sydney Omarr's Astrology, Love, Sex, and You* (Signet); *Celtic Astrology* (New Page); *Romancing the Tarot* (Fireside); *Power Tarot*, coauthored with Trish MacGregor (Fireside); and *Numerology for Baby Names* (Dell). Phyllis resides in Miami, Florida, where she is currently working on her next book, *Erotic Astrology: Secrets of Romantic and Sexual Compatibility*. She can be contacted through her Web site, www.geocities.com/phyllisvega.

**Zach Wong** was born in multicultural Malaysia and brought up in a world full of varying customs, superstitions, and multiple religious beliefs. In vast contrast to this rich diversity, he migrated with his family to Western-influenced Australia where he found himself immersed in Mediterranean culture and Victorian sensibilities. Having completed a degree in architecture, Zach is now pursuing a career as an artist at a glacial pace while enjoying the challenges life e-mails at him. He is the author/artist of the *Revelations Tarot* (Llewellyn).

# Index

# About the Author

In addition to authoring *The Back in Time Tarot Book* and creating the BIT Method, Janet is a prolific writer and reviewer, having posted more than one thousand reviews and articles to JanetBoyer.com, Amazon.com, and elsewhere. She is the editor of the *2009 Tarot World Annual* (TWM Publishing), as well as an editor at TheTarotChannel.com.

Her articles and reviews have appeared in the print publications *Coffee Magazine, Sedona Journal of Emergence, Mystic Pop Magazine, Edge News,* and *Ancient American Magazine.* On the web, her work has been featured in Planet Lightworker, Children of the New Earth, BellaOnline, Kajama Digest, Timeless Spirit, and elsewhere.

In addition to her writing, she also performs intuitive Tarot readings for a worldwide clientele via email through her website JanetBoyer.com. As a columnist for *Tarot World Magazine,* Janet writes specially created BIT Snapshots for every issue.

She makes her home in Pennsylvania with her husband, son, and two cats.

# Hampton Roads Publishing Company

*... for the evolving human spirit*

HAMPTON ROADS PUBLISHING COMPANY publishes books
on a variety of subjects, including spirituality,
health, and other topics.

**For a copy of our latest trade catalog,** call toll-free,
800-766-8009, or send your name and address to:

HAMPTON ROADS PUBLISHING COMPANY, INC.
1125 STONEY RIDGE ROAD • CHARLOTTESVILLE, VA 22902
e-mail: hrpc@hrpub.com • www.hrpub.com